4/12/11

Wanda

Love and Peace
To you. You are
my Teacher.

Blessings

Love S. Bates

"Remember that the Christian life is one of action; not of speech and daydreams." – St. Vincent Pallotti

What's Cooking in Your Soul

By: Lifestyle Coach
Carol S. Batey

Author of "Parents Are Lifesavers," "In Due Season," and "Poise for the Runway of Your Life"

authorHOUSE®

AuthorHouse™
1663 Liberty Drive
Bloomington, IN 47403
www.authorhouse.com
Phone: 1-800-839-8640

© *2010 Carol S. Batey. All rights reserved.*

No part of this book may be reproduced, stored in
a retrieval system, or transmitted by any means
without the written permission of the author.

First published by AuthorHouse 9/10/2010

ISBN: 978-1-4520-7097-1 (e)
ISBN: 978-1-4520-7096-4 (sc)

Library of Congress Control Number: 2010913622

Printed in the United States of America

This book is printed on acid-free paper.

Because of the dynamic nature of the Internet, any Web addresses or
links contained in this book may have changed since publication and
may no longer be valid. The views expressed in this work are solely those
of the author and do not necessarily reflect the views of the publisher,
and the publisher hereby disclaims any responsibility for them.

Are there destinies that you want to unfold? Now is the time to stir up the secret ingredients of intentional desire, prayer, meditation, imagination, action, faith, trust, and expectation. Are you ready to cook up your dreams? This book is the soul guidebook for you to stir and mix up your soul's passions.

"Carol Batey is a gifted storyteller! She has the ability to entrap you in her life's lessons as well as make her life transparent to her readers. She allows her readers to see the struggles, successes, and biblically-sound principles that she applied to step into her destiny. She has a gift to motivate you and encourage you to begin to look within, reflecting on the solid ingredients that literally make you! You will be given the strength to press toward the mark! I am so proud of this project and the many delicacies that will be prepared and birthed all over the world through these healthy words from Carol Batey! God Bless!"

– Minister David L. Dickerson, Progressive Life Giving Word Cathedral Hillside, IL

"Carol S. Batey's new book, *What's Cooking in Your Soul?*, is delicious, filling and satisfying! She draws from her deep personal experiences and stretches you to grow spiritually by providing tools of meditation, writings, and affirmations. She then tops it all off with healthy, yummy recipes with which to nurture yourself. She has given us the whole cake with the icing on it - dig in and enjoy!"

– Reverend Dyann Woody, Music City Center for Spiritual Living, Brentwood, TN

"Carol Batey, truly led by the Spirit, presents a fascinating and unparalleled way of stirring one's inner being that is captivating. Her style is intriguing, paralleling one's desire to seek wholeness reflected through one's unconditional relationship with God."

– Reverend Brenda Haywood, St. John's Missionary Baptist Church, Clarksville, TN

Table of Contents

Introduction	xiii
Chapter 1 – Jai' Batey, a Soul Connection: My Daughter	**1**
Vibration Cooking - Raspberry, Apple, and Hot Pepper Jam	15
Chapter 2 – Magical Moments with Animals	**19**
Vibration Cooking - Fresh Green Salad	25
Chapter 3 – Life Lessons from My Marriage	**27**
Vibration Cooking - Tomato, Basil, and Cinnamon Jam	39
Chapter 4 – Love Mates and Kindred Spirits	**41**
Vibration Cooking - Stuffed French Toast	51
Chapter 5 – Moving Forward	**53**
Vibration Cooking - Fresh Juice	65
Chapter 6 – Why Aren't You Writing?	**67**
Vibration Cooking - Apple Butter	81
Chapter 7 – Your Project Is Finished, Now What?	**83**
Vibration Cooking - Real Snow Ice Cream	103
Chapter 8 – Changing Our Old Patterns of Thinking to Create New Patterns!	**105**
Vibration Cooking - Low Sugar Harvest Melt Cookies	117
Chapter 9 – Train up a Child	**119**

Vibration Cooking - High Protein Blueberry
Smoothie 145

Chapter 10 – Exercising Your Rights! 147

Vibration Cooking - Low Sugar Oatmeal
Thumbprint Cookies 161

**Chapter 11 – What Have You Been Cooking
in Your Life? 163**

Vibration Cooking - Herbal Tea for Relaxation 175

Chapter 12 – Measuring Your Success 177

Vibration Cooking - Gluten-Free Ginger Snaps 201

**Chapter 13 – The Plants Speak: Yes, You Can
Pamper Yourself 203**

Vibration Cooking - Rosemary, Sage, and
Orange Oil 217

Chapter 14 – Are You a Late Bloomer? 219

Vibration Cooking - A Wholesome Snack 235

Chapter 15 – The Ending of this Book 237

Vibration Cooking - Mango, Lemon, Lemon
Balm, and Mint Herb Ice 247

Dear Reader 249

Bibliography 251

Dedication

This book is dedicated to all those who have crossed my life's path. I am thankful to my children for all of the "lessons" that they have taught to me. I give thanks to God, who is the source and supply of my life.

Introduction

Often, I question what is stirring within my soul, directing my life. Do you feel lost? Are you seeking to find a clear direction? Is it time for you to leave your 9-to-5 job and seek your soul's fulfillment or fulfill your heart's desire? Do you feel that if only you could find that one "secret ingredient," you would be able to succeed with your plans? Search no more. I can tell you where to find the secret ingredient to your life's desires. It lies within your soul. It may be locked away by years of hurt and pain, but if you dig deep enough and learn how to rid yourself of the negative energy and forgive past experiences in your life, you will be able to uncover what you desire.

This book was designed to stir up the passions of your soul and provide answers to the provocative questions about the meaning and purpose of your life. *What's Cooking in Your Soul?* will help you to analyze your life and all of the relationships and situations within it. Are you being placed in situations that make you angry or stressed? Is the temperature of your life too hot? Alternatively, are you feeling left behind and out of date, allowing your temperature to become ice cold? Have you stayed too long in one place and allowed your soul to become overdone and stale? Is your life that of a cookie-cutter person or have you allowed yourself to become the true vision of what God intended you to be? What's cooking in your soul at this moment?

Are you in a similar situation to the one that I was in? Were you married for the majority of your adult life, only to file for divorce? Have you looked for love in all of the wrong places, only to find disappointment and heartbreak? Be honest with yourself and look at the needs of your soul. Imagine that you have a mirror that reflects, not your outside image, but the needs and desires of your soul. Do you like what you see? These needs and desires are often, unknowingly, portrayed through your life and shown in glaring light to those around you. Is there someone in your life at whom you can simply glance and see what they need and desire?

Neale Donald Walsch wrote in his book, *Conversations with God*, "when human love relationships fail (relationships never truly fail except in the strictly human sense that they did not produce what you want), they fail because they were entered into for the wrong reason" (1996, p. 122-123). He states that we often enter into relationships for the wrong reasons because we do not have our priorities set on what is best for our lives.

Most people enter into relationships with an eye toward what they can get out of them, rather than what they can put into them. The purpose of a relationship is to decide what part of yourself you'd like to see 'show up,' not what part of another you can capture and hold. There can be only one purpose for relationships and for all of life: to be and to decide who you really are. It is very important to say that now that your special other has entered your life, you feel complete. Yet the purpose of a relationship is not to have another who might complete you; but to have another with whom you might share your completeness (1996, p. 122-123).

> Walsch goes on to say that the paradox of all human relationships is that "you have no need for a particular other in order for you to experience, fully, Who You Are, and… without another, you are nothing" (1996, p. 123).

I am the mother of six wonderful adult children. Growing up, each had his or her own trials, rebellions, drug addictions, and tribulations. I share these events within this book. Chapter 11 in my third book, *Poise for the Runway of Your Life* (2009), is dedicated to my son, a member of the Special Forces, who used drugs between the ages of 12 and 20. In this book, Chapters 1 and 9 focus on my children, written from the point of view of a parent who has been there.

The purpose of this book is to provide you with a fresh positive perspective on how to move forward in your life and mix yourself a new future. Take a bowl and spoon.

Stir in your favorite ingredients and then read the real life stories within this book. Allow them to rise and use the oven of your soul to bake the ingredients with healing, insight, empowerment, inspiration, grace, ease, abundance, prosperity, health, happiness, and success.

Dear Reader:

It is Sunday, December 6, 2009. I have been up since 5 a.m. writing to you this winter morning. I fixed my fresh vegetable juice and my herbal tea sweetened with raw honey. An incense of rose is burning as soft music plays in the background. As you begin mixing the recipe for your new life, remember, I am no different from you and must continue to mix my ingredients in order to create the life that I desire. You and I shall travel together on our runways to the lives that we desire.

Meditation

Take some cleansing breaths. Release all of the thoughts that have been poured into your soul as if emptying a mixing bowl into the sink in your kitchen. Let go of the fear, doubt, and worry that have kept you from achieving success in your life. These negative vibrations tear at your soul's foundation and cause your mixture to fail to rise. Allow yourself to accept that the laws of the universe are working in your favor.

Envision what you want to stir up within your soul. Can you see it? Can you feel it? How does it taste? Can you believe and expect it? Do you want to write and publish a book? Do you want a big or small family? Is it time to lay down the "mask of self-deception" that comes with working a job that you do not enjoy? Are you ready to climb the ladder to the top or do you want to stay at the bottom, wishing for something greater? Do you have a sacred source into which you can place your trust?

Sit in a receiving posture, much like when in prayer. Open your hands to God and ask the questions above. What are the needs of your soul's yearnings? Meditate on your soul's yearnings. Meditation allows you to see what your soul wants you to see, much like prayer. Envision the thing that you desire the most. Close your eyes and open your mind's eye. Dream your life the way that you want it to be. Give yourself permission to dream. Now, open your eyes and look around the room. Become aware of your surroundings. Feel your dreams and hold them in your mind's eye. Give thanks to God for all that is coming your way. Be happy. So be it.

Sugar and spice are so very nice. When added to your life, they will make everything all right. Blended with the right intentions, efforts, and thoughts, you can stir up all that God has in store for you. Be open to receiving the good that He is sending your way.

Remember, transformation does not happen in one simple step. You can only add one ingredient at a time; the wait may make you frustrated, but know that when the time and temperature are just right, your mixture will bake into the life that you desire. At the end of each chapter of this book, you will find a Vibration Cooking recipe to help you on your journey.

I will leave you with the words of Raymond Holliwell, spiritual author and teacher, as he shares insights from his book, *Working with the Law*.

> Most of us could meet our obligations if it were not for fear of some kind that tells us differently. We hypnotize ourselves into a belief, which incapacitates our power. Fear clouds our vision, it benumbs our faculties, it paralyzes our mental forces, which must be free and active if we are to avert calamity. When man's mind is confused by fear, he is in no condition to accept an opportunity. God does not give us the spirit of fear, but courage and a sound mind (1964, p. 174).

Many Blessings,
Carol S. Batey

"I have had the pleasure of knowing Ms. Batey for a couple of years now, and she is a wonderful person. *What's Cooking In Your Soul?* is one of her best works ever. She truly has a calling in motivating people into whatever their hearts desire. May God continue to bless you, Carol, in all your endeavors. Be blessed….

God is and always will be the answer to all of our problems. I tried several of the meditation processes and they work quite well for me. We must continue to look to God for all the answers of life."

"But seek ye first the Kingdom of God, and his righteousness; and all these things shall be added unto you." Matthew, 6:33

> – Angell Davis, Sabbath Day Keeper, Sabbath Day Church of God in Christ

Chapter 1

Jai' Batey, a Soul Connection: My Daughter

"Thy soul can be thy friend, and thy soul can be thy enemy."

– Bhagavad Gita

Have you ever experienced a magical soul moment? That is when something magical starts to happen in your soul during a relationship with someone, a child, or an animal. In that special moment, did you feel as if you had a remembrance of another journey with the person through time or space? Ernest Holmes, the founder of Religious Science, in his book, *The Science of Mind* (1998), defines the *soul* as a "Creative Medium of Spirit, the Mirror of Mind, for it reflects the forms of thought which are given. The mind can only carry out the orders given, it cannot analyze or reject" (p. 633). It is my belief that once thoughts or feelings are poured into your soul from the Creator, they are carried out by the Spirit. The Spirit works through the soul and the body. In the *New American Webster Handy College Dictionary* (1956), the *soul* is defined as "the spiritual part of man or woman or an emotional feeling expressing deep feelings" (p. 432). As you read Jai's story, you will understand that God gave me the idea to adopt and that thought was carried out by the Spirit.

Kindred Soul Connections

On many occasions, I have been surrounded by a friend or an animal or been in a place where I felt a kindred soul connection. For example, many times I have met someone and just considered him or her a casual friend until we truly began talking. Then, I realized that we were more alike than I had ever imagined and, at times, we were able to talk for hours about any- and everything. Another example can be found in the magic of nature. Have you ever found yourself so enthralled by the world around you that you desired never to leave a certain place? Have you ever experienced that kind of magical energy? Did these experiences make you happy or sad? How did they affect the other person?

We often wear a "mask" of deception that stops us from being who we were created by God to be. When we finally meet that one person and we feel safe enough to remove the mask and be our true selves without any hesitation, our souls are unburdened. How does removing the mask in a safe environment make you feel? Does it make you feel loved and accepted by another and by yourself?

Man in the Mirror

Recently, I went to see *This is It*, the movie based on Michael Jackson's life. At the end of the movie, he sings *Man in the Mirror*, which talks about how everything in our personal life starts with the Man in the Mirror. The mirror is a reflection of our lives. Do you like what you see? We are the only ones who can change our world.

In the following, I will explain how the above ideas came together at once in my life when my husband and I decided to adopt our first child.

The Bond of Parents

"The hand that rocks the cradle is the hand that rules the world."

– William Ross Wallace

As parents, we must decide the best time to bring our children into the world. Before that special day, we must prepare our hearts for the love that we will feel for our child and the bond that we will forge with him or her. This sacred bond of parenthood is cemented forever when we first gaze into our child's eyes.

A Fresh Start

My former husband, Joe, and I raised six children. Our first child's arrival was unique in a way that it was not born of our flesh, but instead of our souls' yearning – a soul connection. After we said "I do," Joe told me that he did not want me to work. Instead, he wanted us to try to have a baby. I was shocked as there had not been any discussion as to this effect before our wedding day. Four years later, we were still without a child as God was in control of our lives and he had deemed it was not the correct time for us to conceive. Then, one day, I felt the urge to look into adopting a child. To my surprise, when I shared this idea with Joe, he readily agreed. Shortly thereafter, we filed an application with Human Services in Nashville to become the parents of a baby or young child. It was February

1981. Our social worker asked us if we would like twins, to which I replied that I did not even know what to do with one baby. (Ironically, later we would conceive twins naturally.)

Once the paperwork was filled out and filed, we went home. That night, I dreamt about the social worker. She appeared in my dream and told me, "Mrs. Batey, in September of this year, 1981, you will get a baby." Excited, I woke up to share the "good news" with Joe. He was not as excited as I was because he did not put the same stock in a woman's dreams, intuition, or gut feelings as I did!

In spite of his doubt, we started to prepare the nursery and bought things for a baby. We were having fun. Five months later, we joined the Mormon Church to learn how to raise our family. I grew up in a dysfunctional family and wanted our children to be taught who they were in relation to God, and have real church lessons to apply to their lives. I also did not want to work outside of the home once we had children. The Mormon Church taught me how to prepare food, encourage myself and others to write and leave a legacy for children, and other essential things necessary for a stay-at-home parent. I also learned to trust in God and deepen my spirituality in the oneness of the Spirit. I did not know that I was made in the image of God until I was 26 years old. Before then, I did not know who I was and why I was created.

The Church also teaches its members to keep a journal in order to leave a legacy for their children. At the time of our baptism on August 28, 1981, I began my journal. I asked the Lord to help us to have a large family and work as missionaries. I prayed daily for God to strengthen my communications with my husband, whom I loved so dearly, and to help me become a God-centered mother.

After joining the Church, I began canning and buying food in bulk in preparation for the day that I would be able to quit my part-time job. Each night, I would have similar dreams of the social worker and her message. Eventually, I began seeing a baby with curly hair in the dreams. Soon, my mom and a friend were also having dreams about the arrival of our baby. I believed in my dreams. I knew the time was near.

Five months after we applied to be considered for adoption, I had a very strange dream that prompted me to call the social worker. I asked her if they had found a child for us. She said that they had almost secured a child for us and were simply waiting for the parent's rights to be terminated. At that time, I began journaling to our baby, who was becoming a reality.

It's September

By the beginning of September, we had not received any additional news about our potential baby. Then, on the last day of the month, September 30, 1981, I received a call at home from the Human Services agency in Nashville. However, I was at the grocery store and missed the call. That agency then called Joe's work and left a message that we had a child ready to bring into our family. That night, we could not sleep for the anticipation and excitement.

The next morning, we called at 8 a.m. sharp. Joe took the day off from work and we headed to the agency's office. The social worker told us that they had a little girl for us. She was 21 months old and living in Memphis. When she showed us the picture, I was in shock as it was a picture of the child that I had dreamt about! The only difference was that this child was older than the child in my dreams. As we learned her story, we realized that in my dream, I was seeing her as she had been when she first entered the system from neglect at 6 months of age.

Seeing that picture was a magical soul moment for us. Nashville's Human Services Office told us that the child had been hard to place because of her age. We could only count our blessings that another family had not been blessed with her before we were given our chance to love her. Later that day, I wrote thanks and praise to the Lord in my journal for providing us with such a wonderful, beautiful child. It was a true blessing to be entrusted with such a life.

The next day, we traveled to Memphis to see our daughter, but were not allowed to bring her home. Instead, we had entered the period of adjustment in which the child needed to become used to us before we were allowed to bring her into our family full time. She had become very attached to the older foster grandparents who had taken her in and they did not want to traumatize her by simply removing her from a situation in which she felt comfortable.

However, as soon as we saw our beautiful baby girl, we could not stop smiling. I remember that I cried and Joe could not speak, he was so excited. We knew that we had found the perfect fit for our family.

Entries from My Journal

Several days later, we brought her to Nashville to see our home and spend the night. The next day, we took her back to Memphis to retrieve her things and allow her to say good-bye to the couple who had fostered her. On October 16, she began staying with us permanently.

That first week, she spent a good portion of the time trying to feel us out and understand who we were. By the second week, she was comfortable enough with us to try to see what she could get away with without getting in trouble. The only problem we had was that she refused to accept the love that her Daddy tried to extend to her. As I wrote in my journal each day, I prayed that it would not take Jai' long to get used to Joe.

Thoughts from My Journal

Unfortunately, her adjustment to our home was not as smooth as we and the Nashville Human Services thought it would be. However, she was ours to keep, teach, and nurture. This was a knowing within my soul. Regardless of any challenges we might have had with her, she was a blessing and our wonderful daughter.

On Sunday, November 30, 1981, Jai' Levette Batey was blessed in the church. Her new name, Jai', was given to her by my Godmother, Yvonne. This blessing occurred during the difficult transition time in which Jai' often acted out as she missed the only parents that she had ever known and loved, the older foster couple. One day, Jai' bit me in front of the social worker. I bit her back so that she could see how it felt. The social worker did not like my reaction and called the next day to tell us that they had placed the wrong child in our home. Immediately, we called a lawyer to receive a consultation of our rights. He told us that we could sue them if they tried to take Jai' from us.

The following are direct excerpts from my journal from that time.

<u>November 30, 1981</u>

> The third week was a cream puff and the next one a dream puff. Around the fifth week, I saw her as a child of God. By the sixth week, she was beautiful.

<u>November 31, 1981</u>

> The social workers are coming over to talk to us about whether they placed the wrong child in our home. I remember my dreams about the curly haired baby.

<u>December 1, 1981</u>

> Thanks, Heavenly Father, for the blessings of our little girl of 22 months. We love her. Joe and I have many burdens on us. I have cried, cursed, prayed, and sometimes I just did not know what to do. Things are looking brighter. In my prayers, I talk to my Father in Heaven. I want to be a very good mother and wife. That is what is important to me. I hope that when Jai' grows up she will want to be the best at everything she does. We know that God sent Jai' to us. Our job as parents is to help her know the Heavenly Father's love. It is my prayer that Jai'

grows up to know the Father in her heart. As I write, my prayer for Jai' is that she learns from her parents what she needs to know about the wonderful things in life.

December 17, 1981

Jai' started saying blessings over her food and her prayers at night. This truly is a sweet reflection.

December 19, 1981

Today is Jai's birthday. She is 2 years old.

December 20, 1981

Today, we held a birthday party for Jai'. Our friends and family attended. She said many times "thank you," "I'm sorry," "love you" and the names of our family and friends. She is such a joy.

December 21, 1981

I need to thank my Heavenly Father. Joe and I have a wonderful family life!

During her first month with us, I noticed that Jai' was academically gifted and talented in organizing her things and the things in the kitchen. When she turned 6, I noticed that she had a remarkable singing voice. Once she was enrolled in school, I entered her in a school-wide singing audition for the school choir. She made the cut and was in choir for two years. She played softball, was a girl scout, and babysat for the neighbors for many years beginning at age 10. She often helped me with her siblings.

We had her intelligence tested and she tested very high. I personally walked her paperwork to the Metro Board of Education where she was enrolled in a school for high achievers. If I had not become involved in the process, she would have gone unnoticed, as she did not receive an invitation to attend either of the gifted schools. At that time, Jai' did not understand the importance of attending one of these schools. Like most kids her age, she rebelled. Eventually, her ability to get into trouble caused me to remove her from the gifted school and enroll her in a different school so that she could attend with her friends. After she had been at this school for a while, the guidance counselor called to say that her scores were so high that she could write her ticket to any college in the world. Shortly thereafter, I re-enrolled her in the gifted school. She now understood the importance of a good education. She graduated with a 4.0 and was given a full scholarship to college where she graduated with another 4.0. She now lives in a major city where she works for an insurance company. Jai' enjoys the life that God has given her with her adoptive family and does not desire to search for her birth parents.

National Adoption Day is November 21st of every year. If you are considering adopting a child, you should visit your local Human Services Office. Right now, many boys are waiting to be adopted. Potential adoptive parents should remember that, as with any child, raising an adopted child will come with its own struggles and obstacles. These struggles or obstacles may double if you adopt a "hard to place" child as these children have often faced obstacles, health challenges, and neglect in their life and require extra attention. However, do not let this term deter you as these children often have a great capacity to love and have the potential to be spectacular members of society, if given the proper chance. If you are unsure as to whether you are ready to adopt a child, consider first becoming a foster parent. As Jai's parents, we chose to tell her that she was adopted, instead of keeping this information from her. It has been my experience that when you keep important information like that from the child it comes back to haunt you and the child forever.

Meditation

If you would like to increase the size of your family, you must first meditate on this fact in order to bring yourself into harmony with your soul's desires. Ask yourself "Why do I want to increase my family?" Then, ask, "How do we want our family to look?"

Do you understand the concept of meditation? According to Isaac Disraeli, meditation allows one to "[turn] the eye of the mind inwards…form an artificial solitude; [retire] amidst a crowd, [be] calm amidst distraction, and wise amidst folly" (Frank, 2001, p. 499). If your desires are to increase your family's size, you must envision what you desire in order to make your dreams come true. Start journaling about the type of family that you would like to create. Journaling will help you to focus and make your dreams into reality. So be it.

Vibration Cooking

Here is what's cooking from Vibration Cooking. Vibration Cooking does not use measurements. Instead, you simply rely on your intuition and taste! Get in tune with your soul and intuition and see what happens.

Raspberry, Apple, and Hot Pepper Jam

Ingredients
A large handful of raspberries
5 chopped or grated apples with the cores and skins removed
A handful of chopped green peppers
A handful of chopped banana peppers
A handful of chopped large red peppers
2 chopped jalapeño peppers (optional)
A handful of basil leaves
2 handfuls of brown sugar

Place in pot with enough water to cover and simmer on low heat for two hours.

My sister takes this jam and adds a handful of grated cheese on the top. Then, she spreads it on warm whole wheat or rye toast! This lovely jam can also be eaten with cream cheese and crackers. My dear friend put this jam on her Thanksgiving turkey.

The jam can be canned if you wish to store it for long periods. You can place it in the refrigerator if it is to be eaten shortly after being made.

This jam is food for the soul and spirit. It will help you keep in touch with what you are trying to create in your life. It also goes great with a cup of peppermint and lemon herb tea with honey in it. You will become relaxed as you drink this tea and dream of your new family.

If you are still not relaxed and able to meditate, I recommend a sea salt, Epsom salt, and baking soda bath or a refreshing Swedish massage! While enjoying either a bath or massage, make sure to envision what you want in a family.

Use this space to jot down your positive thoughts. If you could have one wish from God, what would it be? Do not be afraid to dream!

_____

_____

_____

_____

_____

_____

_____

What's Cooking in Your Soul

_____

_____

_____

_____

And so it is!

Chapter 2

Magical Moments with Animals

"May today there be peace within. May you trust that you are exactly where you are meant to be. May you not forget the infinite possibilities that are born of faith in yourself and others. May you use the gifts that you have received, and pass on the love that has been given to you. May you be content with yourself just the way you are. Let this knowledge settle into your bones, and allow your soul the freedom to sing, dance, praise, and love. It is there for each and every one of us."

– St. Theresa's Prayer *(As Known by Little Flower)*

A dear friend of mine, whose spiritual faith lies in the Unity movement, volunteered for the betterment of animals for over 25 years before she finally saw her act of demonstration. The word *demonstration* as defined in *The Ernest Holmes New Thought Dictionary* by philosopher and founder of Religious Science Ernest Holmes, is "any objective manifestation which takes place as a result of conscious inner awareness" (1991, p. 32). She has been a great mediator for animal rights for many years. After seeing the injustices done to animals, she vowed to show compassion and educate others on why they too should show compassion to these creatures. During her 25 years, she volunteered her time, talents, and means to many animal rights organizations. While working a full-time job, she personally rescued and found forever homes for many animals. She has even adopted ten cats and a dog into her own family.

After many years of rescuing animals from abuse and neglect at the local level, she felt the call to help them at the state level. This call came from deep within her soul and she knew it was her calling in life. Do you know your own calling? God planted within her soul a deeper desire to help and a larger vision of what the world could be.

Once she felt the desire to take her mission to the state level, her spirit began to stir. She tapped into the Mind of God and used the "Law of Attraction" to manifest her dreams. *The Law of Attraction* is defined in *The Ernest Holmes New Thought Dictionary* as "the principle that we attract that to which our thought is attuned" (Holmes, 1991, p. 77). The Law of Attraction simply means that whatever you set your strongest thoughts or desires on will be attracted to you. Bishop E. Bernard Jordon stated in his book *The Laws of Thinking* that "the key to manifestations is focusing your attention powerfully and persistently on what you desire" (2006, p. 32).

The Missing Link

In order to achieve her goal, she meditated on the problem. She then constructed a strategy on the "missing link" necessary to bring awareness to Georgia about the rights of animals. After three years, she ran into an animal rights lawyer with whom she shared her visions. He told her to write a proposal of what was needed in order to make her vision a reality and submit it to the Humane Society of the United States (HSUS). Using this proposal, she stepped through the doors that God opened to her in order to improve society for the betterment of the animals. What dreams or goals do you wish to create for yourself? Can you give yourself permission to dream?

Using the Gift of Writing

When she wrote her proposal, no positions were available. She then used her creative mind and tapped into the Mind of God to write her proposal to increase the position's prominence. After a high-level individual at Humane Society of the United States read the proposal, she was invited to attend a conference where she met the Vice President of HSUS. The Vice President took her hand and told her that the proposal she wrote was exactly what the state needed. She then informed her that a position for the Georgia State Director for the Humane Society of the United States was available and that she should apply for it. The Holy Bible says that you need to "write the vision and make it plain" (Habakkuk 2:2, NKJV). She wrote her plan, made it plain, and succeeded toward her goals simply because she trusted in God and allowed Him to lead her life and destiny.

Bishop E. Bernard Jordan states in *The Laws of Thinking* that in order to manifest your deep desires, you need to understand the power of writing. Once you set your goals, you need to put them in writing, because, according to Jordan, "when you write about the same thing [your goals], you make it five times more likely to happen" (2006, p. 44). He also states that writing your goals allows you to organize your thoughts in ways that you could not do through speech and "when you sit down to write out the things you desire or what you intend to create, that is making a pact with God" (p. 46). Once you have placed your goals on paper, your goals should come to fruition using the Law of Attraction.

"Writing is the entry point of Spirit into Matter."
– Bishop E. Bernard Jordon

The result of my friend's vision is that the animal laws of her state are changing and she is now the Georgia State Director for the Humane Society of the United States. "Ask and ye shall receive" (Matthew 7:7, NKJV).

We often make too many excuses for why we do not answer the call to follow the passions of our heart. Yet, when someone else follows the passions of their hearts, we become jealous, bitter and, sometimes, defensive. We all have our own missions to fulfill. What are yours? Are you willing to open your mind and heart in order to hear the Divine thoughts of God? Have you written down your vision and goals?

Below is an affirmation, or statement of positive truth, that I created for you to use if you desire a new job, life plan, or project:

Today, I welcome all of the gifts of the Universe to create all that I desire. I will write my vision and make it plain as I wait for God. So it is.

As I continue to fulfill my mission, I will eat healthy foods, such as raw celery with hummus and nuts. I will drink fresh carrot, celery, spinach, and apple juices in order to replenish my body, mind, and soul. This fresh juice will give me the energy and vitamins necessary to wait to hear God's voice.

I trust that I am exactly where God meant for me to be. I will not forget the infinite possibilities that are born of faith, as St. Theresa suggests. Amen.

"I think dogs are the most amazing creatures; they give unconditional love.
For me they are the role model for being alive."
– Gilda Radner (Taste of Life, 2009)

Meditation

Clear your mind. What would you like to create in your life? Would you like a new job, home, or soul mate? Visualize what you want. Feel it in your heart and soul. Believe that you can achieve it. Keep that image in your mind and act upon your feelings. Believe that you can achieve it and it will be so.

Vibration Cooking

Fresh Green Salad

<u>Ingredients</u>
Fresh greens
Vegetables
Handful of nuts
Handful of raisins or dried cranberries
Lemon juice from 2 lemons
Maple syrup
Olive oil

Cut your fresh greens. Add any fresh vegetables that you would like on your salad. Add a handful of nuts. Add a handful of raisins or dried cranberries.

To make the dressing, mix the juice from two freshly squeezed lemons with maple syrup to taste and olive oil.

Chapter 3

Life Lessons from My Marriage

"By marriage, the husband and wife are one person in law: that is, the very being or legal existence of the woman is suspended during marriage, or at least incorporated and consolidated into that of the husband.... But though our law in general considers man and wife as one person, yet there are some instances in which she is separately considered; as inferior to him, and acting by his compulsion."

– William Blackstone

Everyone perceives an event or situation differently. This chapter is based on my perception of the events that occurred in my marriage and is not intended to hurt or offend anyone. It was simply created to share the lessons that I have learned. Is that not what life is all about? Learning and growing?

My 21-year marriage had many difficulties, as any marriage is bound to have. However, each of my painful situations taught me a little bit more about myself and who I wanted to be. I have found that the best medicine for one's life is to look back on and forgive yourself for past regrets. Forgiveness, letting go, and learning from each of the situations in your life are the only ways by which you will be able to move forward.

You may choose to rewrite your past in order to discover a positive outcome. I have undertaken such exercises in my life in order to take responsibility for my actions and freely let go of negative emotions. I may cry, but I take the time to see the issues at hand clearly. Then, I ask my Higher Power and Higher-self what gifts I have gained from the lesson taught to me. We are on this Earth to grow, develop spirituality, help others along their paths, and use such exercises to allow this growth to happen.

Victim vs. Victor

The troubled times in my marriage taught me to recognize controlling and negative behavior in others. This ability led to a lesson that I learned on how not to be a victim. Even now, I still occasionally fall into negative relationships, not only with men, but also in my friendships with women. Often, when you are in an unhealthy relationship, you tend to lose yourself, your spirit, and your soul. If you want to achieve your dreams, you cannot allow yourself to stay in such situations. Only by becoming proactive and taking control of your life can you break out of these situations, discover who you are, and achieve your dreams. Unfortunately, it took 19 years for me to learn this lesson and I am still traveling on the journey to recovery.

Men Who Hate Women and the Women Who Love Them

During the last few years of my marriage, I was emotionally abused, of which I was not fully aware until a professional marriage counselor brought it to my attention. He told me to read *Men Who Hate Women and the Women Who Love Them* by Susan Forward and Joan Torres, which is available in most public libraries.

According to the counselor and the book, I was not standing up for my rights and allowing myself to be the person who I could and should be. I allowed myself to be held down because I believed that the one holding me down loved me and was doing it with my best interests at heart. By allowing myself to be held down in an abusive situation, I was allowing myself to be held back from the things that I felt I should be doing. I did not know that I had rights!

While this knowledge was enlightening, it did not convince me to leave my marriage. It was not until the emotional abuse turned to physical abuse and the physical abuse turned to abuse toward my children that I stood up and said, "No more." One day, I told him that if he yelled at me again, I would kill him and go to prison. It was the first time that I had ever stood up to him.

In these types of situations, the woman often looks for some way to punish the man. I did not want anything to do with my husband anymore, so I stopped all of my relationships with him: sexual, physical, and emotional. However, I was not trying to punish him. I just wanted him to leave me alone. I did not feel emotionally safe anymore.

Abuse Can Be Confusing

During this time, our relationship became very confusing. He would leave the house and then later call and ask if I wanted to go to dinner. This routine was starting to make me hate men and I realized that I needed to escape the prison that he and I had created together. I prayed to God to give me a job that I could do for the rest of my life. At that time, I was working as a part-time parent consultant for a local school system, but it was not enough to pay the bills.

A few days later, I went to get a massage and a thought popped into my head, "I could do this!" I came home and shared the news with Joe, who angrily told me, "How are you going to pay for [the training]?" I told him that if God wanted me to attend massage school, then he would create a way for me to attend. That way came in the form of a school loan. During the nine months that I was in school, I was still experiencing emotional abuse. I only persevered because God's grace was surrounding and protecting me. Shortly after I graduated from massage school, I filed for divorce from Joe.

Gaining Strength outside of Myself

After I filed for divorce, I decided that I no longer wanted to live in the home that we had built. My attorney managed to win monthly financial allotments from Joe while I still lived with him until everything was final. These allotments allowed me to begin looking for a new place for me and our children to live. Leaving the old home behind was freeing and allowed me to learn about myself and what I was capable of doing on my own.

At that time, Joe filed for custody of all five of our underage children. However, the judge refused his request, stating that Joe was handicapped and unable to care for the children. The judge said that if we could not decide on the children's living arrangements on our own, she would split them up. Joe was furious that he was not in control and could not alter the situation, but in the end, we agreed on the children's living arrangements.

My Divorce Began My Spiritual Transformation

What was cooking in my soul? It contained hidden messages to be unfolded. I opened myself up to hear and see so that I could be reborn into who I needed to be. My divorce was the beginning of my freedom and my spiritual and personal transformation. I had already moved into a new home and was ready to start my new life.

The Negative Words Rang in My Soul

The verbal and emotional abuse that I had sustained during our marriage still rang in my ears every morning when I woke up. After a while, it began to affect my ability to move on. One day, a voice inside me told me to write down the negative things that I remembered and answer them with a positive statement about myself.

For example, Joe had told me that once I experienced the real world, I would come back to him, and that I must change to fit his will and desires. My answer to this controlling statement was: "I always took care of the bills for our home and children. I am not afraid to venture out by myself." What Joe did not realize was that our divorce was not completely about him. It was also about reclaiming my freedom and learning about me. I needed to uncover who I was and what my purpose was in life. I did so much in our marriage for him and the children that I had neglected the person underneath the wife and mother. It was time for that woman to fight her way to the surface and shine.

You may also have negative words ringing in your soul from a relationship that did not allow you to exercise and free yourself. Using the above method might help you as well.

Two weeks after the divorce was finalized, I dropped the children off at my ex-husband's house for his parenting time. He told the children to come in and meet his girlfriend. The children were shocked because they did not know that he had been seeing anyone. I was even more shocked when it turned out that I knew the woman, as she was the cousin of one of my friends. I was hurt that my friend must have known what was going on, but never told me.

Six months later, he and his girlfriend were married. Shortly thereafter, I brought them a bottle of wine to congratulate them. They were shocked, but it was a step that I had to take in order to move on with my life.

In Time All Wounds Are Healed

In time, all wounds are healed. By choosing to forgive, letting go, and moving forward, you will be able to find the silver lining in every situation. I can now look back on the times when I felt alone after the divorce and know that I was never truly alone. I always had God there with me, helping me change, and providing me with comfort.

I had never had close relationships with men before I was married. After my divorce, I realized that I wanted a male friend simply to go to dinner or the movies with. One of my friends introduced me to a man named Scott Beatty, with whom I went to dinner. I was intrigued as his last name is pronounced the same way as mine. We did not hit it off and I did not think that I would see him again.

Unfortunately, I realized that I did not know how to date or be with a man other than my ex-husband.

Two weeks later, Scott left a message on my answering machine asking me to dinner that Sunday afternoon. I was shocked. After church, I met up with him. At the end of the evening, he asked me if he could kiss me. I was quite nervous for two reasons. First, he was a white man and second, he was not my ex-husband. After he kissed me, I looked into his eyes and realized that he was the man about whom I had been having dreams. In these dreams, I felt safe and comfortable. Once again, God had led me to exactly where I needed to be.

As time went by, almost every time that I thought of him, he would call. I later learned that these coincidences were actually the result of the Law of Attraction, which occurs when the dominant thought held in your mind is attracted by other like thoughts. I felt so comfortable with him, completely at ease. It is because of him that I now believe in past life occurrences. My soul knew him from another place and time.

Until meeting him, I did not think that another man would ever love me again, which was a self-created limitation that I had imposed on my life. I could not have been more wrong. A friend once told me that people come into your life for a reason, season, or lifetime, as all relationships can provide us with learning experiences and growth. This relationship taught me about setting healthy relationship boundaries for myself in order to learn how to give and receive love. It also taught me that it takes more than one person to make a relationship work. Relationships are about balancing give and take. I had blamed myself for my marriage failing, but I now realized that the fault did not lie entirely on my shoulders.

The New Friendship

My relationship with my new friend lasted for about three years before I decided to end it. I wanted to date him exclusively and he did not wish to make the same commitment. While he and I were the same age, he had never been married nor had children and wanted his freedom. Therefore, I decided that it was time to move on to the next stage of my life.

This period in life was also a time of spiritual transformation for me in regard to how to understand God and other people. I turned to an old sage for advice who told me to visit a New Thought church, such as Unity or the Center for Spiritual Living (which was called Religious Science at that time). At first, I was unsure, as I did not know what a New Thought church was. According to Holmes, in *The Ernest Holmes New Thought Dictionary*, *New Thought* is "a system of thought, which affirms the unity of God and man, the perfection of all life and the immortality and eternality of the individual soul forever expanding" (1991, p. 99).

Maybe your story is similar to mine or maybe you were simply in a situation in which you felt trapped or held down, a prisoner in your own skin. I have found that writing my story has not only helped others, but also helped myself to heal. Do you keep a journal of your wishes, desires, and daily activities? I love to journal my thoughts. Often, I will look back at previous entries to see how far I have come from where I have been, performing my own life review. Today, I can look back on my life in my marriage and see how much I have grown, emotionally and spiritually. I hope that my story helps you do the same for your life.

Meditation

My dears, we are all prisoners of some deception that exists in our lives. It is up to us to face the truth and work toward removing our masks in order to walk in the freedom of being who God made us to be. This process is called walking in our truth and claiming our entitlement to our God-self. You and I can find our God-selves if we look into our souls to see the images presented for us to see. Do not be afraid to look inside yourself to find the better you. What's cooking in your soul? There is a better you to find if only you remain true!

Today, I walk near the water to wash my soul's memory, while renewing my faith in God, humanity, and myself. As the air blows through my hair, I will become cleansed by nature. I will forgive God, myself, and others who I think caused me pain or harm. I will become lighter. I will lay down my baggage and leave it outside of my soul. I will take my shoes off and walk on the stones. Barefooted, I will feel nature renewing my path. I will see the footprints of God who has gone before me to help create new events and situations in my life. I will lay down the mask of being a prisoner of others and myself. I will affirm that I am free. Let the newness begin today.

As you walk barefoot near the water, feel the sun against your skin. Can you feel it? Can you see the sun's glowing reflection against your warm skin? The sun makes us relax and massages our inner bodies as well as our outside form. It warms our cells, blood, organs, and tissues so that they can work in harmony. This harmony connects all parts of your body in order to make you one with God and the self that God wishes you to be. You are vibrant and alive with no memory of past events, just lessons learned. Amen.

Vibration Cooking

Tomato, Basil, and Cinnamon Jam

<u>Ingredients</u>

A pinch of cinnamon

A handful of washed and cored tomatoes

6-10 chopped basil leaves

The juice from 2 lemons

Splenda

Water to fill the pan

Cook on low heat for about two hours.

I love to add this jam to my spaghetti sauce and chili. Add it to your favorite tomato-based sauce for a new twist.

Chapter 4

Love Mates and Kindred Spirits

"If you would be loved, love and be loveable."
– Benjamin Franklin (1706-1790)

During the years since my divorce, many of my friends have asked me to write a relationship book. I had often told them stories about my dating experiences and the kindred spirits that I have found within some of the men that I have dated. However, each time I have declined, unknowingly setting self-imposed limitations on myself. In the end, I shrugged off these limitations and wrote this chapter. It is completely true, except for the names, which have been changed. My hope for you as you read this chapter is that you will gain insights into your own relationships. During most of the stories in this chapter, I was newly divorced and still in search of who I am.

Avoiding Love Mate Pitfalls

New York Times bestselling author Sylvia Browne states in her book Sylvia Browne's Lessons for Life, that while it is fine to base a relationship on chemistry, it is very important to also have communication, understanding, trust, patience, and respect (2004, pp. 86-88).

She also points out that in a healthy relationship, each partner accepts the other for who he or she is and does not try to change him or her. "And please know that you can't change someone with an addiction, whether it's to sex, drugs, or alcohol" (2004, p. 87). To her list, I am adding addictions to work, status, control, or money.

What's Cooking in Your Soul

I wish that I had been given this advice 12 or even 40 years ago so that I could have avoided many of the pitfalls that have occurred in my life.

According to Browne, you do not want to become involved with individuals who have a *reflective personality*. Individuals with this type of personality often reflect their guilt onto another person. For example, I once dated a man I really liked; however, he kept thinking that I was seeing other people. In reality, he was seeing other people and was reflecting his guilt upon me instead of accepting it for himself.

Have you ever met a person who likes everything you like, making it appear that you are soul mates or kindred spirits, and then you find out that they were simply *lifeless-lump personalities*? As defined in Browne's book, this type of person feigns interest in everything you are interested in because they do not have their own unique personality.

You should also avoid *misogynists*. Unfortunately, I have encountered more than one of these individuals in my life. A *misogynist* hates, dislikes, or mistrusts women. Browne states that a female version of this type of personality also exists. In fact, I know many women who think that they like men, but really only want their money or for the man to buy them presents. These individuals suffer from *misandry*, or a hatred of men. Do you fall into this category?

Have you ever dated someone who thinks that they are or should be the most important thing in your life? Browne stated that these individuals have an *undeveloped personality*. This type of personality is immature and pretends that they cannot do anything on their own. The author shares that "deep down, they're not only lazy, but they also have the prince or princess aura" (2004, p.88).

The final personality type that you should avoid, according to Browne, is the *jealous and insecure personality*. I was married to a man with this personality for 21 years. These types of individuals feel as if you should wait on them, buy them presents, and fulfill their every wish. They want to control what you are doing at all times and will ask questions such as "What time are you returning?," "Where are you going?," and "Who are you going with?" Both men and women are known to fall within this category. Many individuals who have this type of personality do not feel that you should have your own unique identity.

Love Mate Attractions

Shortly after my divorce, I started investigating New Thought churches and the movement behind them. I also wanted to meet someone who might want more than simple companionship. My custody agreement with my ex-husband allowed me to have my children every other week. During the weeks that I did not have my children, I was able to discover my gifts, talents, and abilities.

It was then that I began attending an herbal school in Atlanta, Georgia. When I was 26, I began studying herbal medicine. As I am one-third American Indian, herbal knowledge is near and dear to my heart. American Indians have used herbs since the beginning of their history and taught the settlers this knowledge as well. As I raised my children, I incorporated herbs into our daily use and diet. You should hear them talk about their experiences while growing up, but now they often call me to ask me for a "home remedy."

After I became divorced and completed my massage therapy studies, I decided that I wanted to have a better understanding of the properties of plants. At the age of 45, I became a licensed skincare professional in Tennessee. Today, I use my knowledge to create skincare products to use in my daily life. Within this book, I will share several of my skincare recipes. In addition, on my website (http://www.artlifestylecoach.com), I write a newsletter called *The Plants Speak*, in which I discuss how best to use plants in our daily lives.

My Connection to God Was Missing

I still felt as if something was missing from my life. I thought I needed a man to make me feel complete, so I placed a personal ad in the newspaper. It was from this ad that I met Sam A. He was short and quite handsome and we went out to dinner. We quickly became friends, but I realized that he was not the man for whom I had been searching. I was not sure of who or what I was really looking for as I had never written down exactly what I wanted in a man. At that time, I did not know that I should make a list and check it twice!

He was lonely and needed a friend. His beloved dog had recently died and I spent many nights just spending time with him. I was at his house so often that one of my girlfriends stated that she thought I was going to move in with him and, in fact, I almost did.

One day, I loaned him a CD of New Thought artist Rickie Byars Beckwith's music in order to introduce him to her music, not realizing that she was married to Reverend Michael Beckwith of the Agape Church, or that this connection would prove to be very important in the future. Sam A. loved the music.

Eventually, I decided to end the relationship. When I tried to stop our friendship, he was not happy. I blocked his home number from my house phone, but then he called me on his cell phone. I stopped answering that number as well. When I stopped answering his phone calls, he came to the place at which I was giving massages to try to see me. I hid in the kitchen until he left. While our chemistry was great, I wanted to move forward with my life, and he was stuck in his. In order to move forward with my goals, I had to disconnect myself from him and focus on the desires of my soul. In Rickie Byars Beckwith's song *All I Needed Was My Connection with God*, she sings, "I used to think that I needed somebody and all I needed was my connection with God." These lyrics fit perfectly with my life at that time.

Relationships teach us about ourselves if we allow the other person to mirror our reflections. Often, when we start to see a pattern in the reflections, we run.

Hiding from Sam A.

The day after Sam came to my place of work, I felt guilty about hiding from him. Two days later, I went to the Nashville Center for Spiritual Living and Sam was there. I spent a good portion of the time at the church on the opposite side of the building, trying to stay away from him. When the service was over, he found me and begged me to go to lunch with him.

Do you understand the Law of Attraction? I went to lunch with him that day and we have stayed friends ever since. Today, we laugh together about our lives. He reminds me of a brother, as if he is an old soul connection. Have you ever experienced such a connection that you just could not explain?

The Mirror of Reflections and Lessons Learned

"But we all, with unveiled face, beholding as in a mirror the glory of the Lord, are being transformed into the same image from glory to glory, just as by the Spirit of the Lord."

– 2 Corinthians 3:18, KJV

We all have soul mates whose wants and desires mirror those of our own soul, who we can simply embrace into our lives and to whom we instantly feel close. This bond allows you to share everything with the other person without a moment's hesitation. To me, Sam was one such person. Many times, he kept me from becoming too jaded about the world around me and kept my heart from being like stone, unable to accept love. He allowed my heart to stay open to the flow of love from the source of all things.

Four years after I met Sam, he moved from Nashville to Los Angeles. One day after church, he called me and said, "Guess who was playing the piano today?" I asked, "Who?" He responded, "Rickie Byars Beckwith!" I told him that I would come to visit him and attend church

What's Cooking in Your Soul

with him the next week. Although he bought me a ticket to come to LA, I never made the trip.

Sam told me about the message that Reverend Beckwith preached that day. (I discuss this message in more detail in Chapter 2 of my second book, *In Due Season: Destiny Is Calling Your Soul*, 2007.) The topic was that you are never too old to live your dreams. Sam moved to LA after watching *The Secret*, which focuses on how the Law of Attraction has been used by many over time. At the age of 52, he decided that he would spend 30 days trying to fulfill his dream of becoming an actor. To date, he has had many auditions and been in several movies. In addition, he also became a trained massage therapist at the age of 54 and sings in the Agape International Choir, a prestigious honor, as you must audition before being accepted.

Meditation

This day, I allow my heart to open to all of the possibilities of love. Love is the highest vibration on this Earth. I welcome love. In order to accept love, I must first forgive and love myself. I must accept the image I see in the mirror of the person that God has made. I am made of love because God is love and I was made in His image. God is a verb, an action, not a noun. His love will help me to love and accept myself, today and every day following. Always remember that God is a God of action.

I will write down what I desire in a love mate. I will focus on the aspects of a love relationship that I desire, not on what I do not desire. I will focus on what my soul wants, not on any preconceived notions placed into my head by others. I will forgive all of the individuals with whom I have had relationships that ended in a negative manner. I will send rays of love from my heart to theirs. I will repeat this mantra:

I love you. I forgive you. Can you forgive me for any hurt that I have caused you?

Allow yourself to move forward, past any transgressions made against you or that you have made. Do not carry guilt and shame in your heart. It will only weigh down your soul.

Light an incense of champak. Close your eyes and empty your mind. Imagine that you are walking next to the ocean with your beloved. See your beloved take your hand in a gesture of love and affection. Feel your souls become one. Walk together next to the footprints of God. Allow your combined soul to become one with God. So be it.

Vibration Cooking

Stuffed French Toast

If you desire a love mate, close your eyes before you begin and imagine him or her making this recipe with you.

Ingredients

2 eggs

Soymilk

Cinnamon

Allspice

Vanilla

Loaf of potato bread

Olive oil

Pineapple cream cheese

Walnuts

Strawberry jam

Beat two eggs in a bowl. Add soymilk, cinnamon, allspice, and vanilla. Mix well.

Place the strawberry jam, pineapple cream cheese, and walnuts on top of the bread. Then, place another piece of bread on top of this creation.

Place olive oil in a skillet. Heat the skillet. Dip the bread into the mixture and place it into the heated skillet. Brown the toast on both sides.

Put fresh flowers on the table. Fill two wine glasses with fresh orange juice and two fresh mint leaves. Set places for you and your love mate. At your love mate's table setting, place a note that says, "I'm so glad that you came." As you eat your meal, practice having a conversation with your love mate. Practice makes perfect! Use your imagination!

Affirmation

You are loved. God is nothing, but love. I am love and so are you. Amen.

Chapter 5

Moving Forward

"Love is, above all, the gift of oneself."
– Jean Anouilh (1910-1987)

Have you noticed the number of families torn apart by divorce, dysfunctional dynamics, or the death of a spouse? Children in today's society often grow up in single-parent homes or homes with stepparents. Men and women remarry without any thought to the children involved. Too often, the rules and boundaries of the parent's dating relationship or new marriage are not set because neither party has thought about the children involved or the blended families that will be created. Many men and women cannot stand to live alone and rush to get married or live with someone. Often, the children resent the parent's decision as these parents or their new spouses feel that children should be seen and not heard. I, however, am of a different mindset when making decisions that will affect my entire family.

No Need to Rush into Marriage

In our culture, single parents are often pressured to remarry. If they do not remarry, family members and friends question them as to why they have not done so, essentially putting more pressure on them, which makes them feel inadequate. However, they are not inadequate because, contrary to society's thinking, one does not need another person in order to be whole.

My Story

I have been happily divorced for 12 years. I have heard on TV talk shows that I am one of 80% of women who do not remarry after the death of a spouse or a divorce. This morning, a woman asked me why I was not married. After I laughed, I told her that I am taking time to know and understand who I am in my relationship with God. I need to understand my ultimate purpose on Earth and how I may serve the sacred source. In addition, it takes two to form a relationship; both parties must be in an agreement and in alignment.

> *"Then, the Lord God said it is not good that the man should be alone;*
> *I will make him a helper who is like him."*
> *– Genesis 2:18, KJV*

After my divorce, I did not want a new husband in the home in which I was raising my children. This choice was a conscious one made so that my children's lives would not be disrupted any more than they already had been. In my third year of being single, a gentleman friend asked for my hand in marriage. I told him that the time was not right. I needed to wait until my children were grown and were no longer living in my home. The man I was dating could not accept this answer and ended the relationship. Six years later, we reconnected and he asked me again. Once again, I said no, but this time it was simply because I did not love him in that way. I know of single mothers and fathers who rush into new marriages because they need help with their household bills. These marriages often suffer because the individuals get married for the wrong reasons. Then, they stay in these relationships solely because they fear being alone, rather than taking the time to find the right person before remarrying.

Live Your Life without Regrets

In such relationships as the ones described above, the parties often experience regrets later in life because they rushed into the situation without first getting to know the other person or the children involved. I have known women who have married men with children and then chose not to interact with their stepchildren. These women are bitter and unhappy because they realize that they have not gotten what they thought they would get out of the relationship.

If you are involved in a relationship with someone with children, please realize that your relationship not only affects you and your partner, but your partner's children as well. You need to get to know these children and understand their needs. If you are dating or planning to marry a single parent, make sure your decisions are in the best interests of the children. If they are not, then you should not undertake them. You need to make sure that your partner is not simply in the relationship because of money issues, out of loneliness, for status reasons, or because society has deemed it required.

Being alone by choice is an acceptable choice. I am alone by choice despite society's expectations. While I have occasionally sought out the companionship of another, I also have the freedom to travel and visit others as I please. I can visit my children and help them with tasks, such as painting or cooking, without having to report my activities to another person. I am the master of my life. For example, as I write this chapter, it is 4 a.m. on Christmas morning in 2009. My grandbaby, stepfather, friends, and children and their spouses were over to my house last night. It is possible to live a completely fulfilling life without a partner.

Don't Believe Everything You Hear

Have you ever run into a man or woman who tells their new spouse negative stories about their previous spouse? Unfortunately, the new spouse never gets to hear the previous spouse's side of the story. Usually, half of what the new spouse is saying is untrue, as there are two sides to every story. In the end, all these stories do is force the new spouse to create an opinion of the old spouse based on negative half-truths. If you are in this position, I suggest that you keep an open mind as your new spouse tells you negative stories about their previous spouse. Also, it is important to not dwell on the past and, instead, live in the present and plan for the future.

Move Forward and Release Your Guilt

In some cases, one spouse may feel guilty about how he or she formed his or her current relationship. Maybe the person was having one or more affairs and, after his or her divorce was final, he or she got remarried. Now, every time he or she sees the former spouse, he or she feels guilty. This feeling is called the mirror of reflection. You need to remember that this problem is owned by the spouse who had the affair. The best way to proceed is to simply move forward. Do not try to blame your former spouse. Instead, teach yourself forgiveness.

In order to get past this guilt, we must learn to forgive. As we learn to forgive, we improve our faith. If we choose not to forgive, we cannot move past our emotional pain and our faith cannot be restored. Thus, we will simply continue to cause pain and damage to our soul, which can lead to the growth of disease within your body, such as high blood pressure, cancer, or headaches.

Below is an exercise that will help you learn how to forgive.

What's Cooking in Your Soul

Write a letter below to the person from whom you would like forgiveness. Ask them to forgive you for your mishaps and harmful actions. Tell them that you love them and wish them happiness. Imagine the person surrounded by the white light of the Holy Spirit. Wish them well on their life's journey. Restoration is for all who seek it.

_____

_____

_____

_____

_____

_____

_____

_____

_____

_____

So it is.

James Allen, in his book *As a Man Thinketh*, quoted in the *Prosperity Bible*, discusses the calmness of mind.

How many people we know who sour their lives, who ruin all that are sweet and beautiful by explosive tempers, which destroy their poise of character, and make bad blood? How few people we meet in life who are well balanced, who have that exquisite poise which is characteristic of the finished character! (Hill, et al, 2007, p. 237)

Do you desire to be balanced and complete?

A Change on the Inside Affects the Outside

Recently, during a Sunday church service, our pastor, Reverend Chuck Thomas spoke of "A Change on the Inside." As he spoke, I thought about how holding ill feelings within you, such as regret, envy, hatred, and guilt, can cause you to become ill. For example, according to *Webster's New World Dictionary* (1970), the definition of *cancer* is "a malignant tumor, which can spread and ulcerate" (p. 69). The same dictionary defines *malignant* as "very harmful" (p. 285). The beginning of the word *malign* means "to speak slander of, defame, having an evil disposition toward others, tending to injure" (p. 285). Moving forward and practicing forgiveness starts with you. What are your thoughts toward harmful situations, others, and yourself? Do you exhibit love toward yourself and others? Do you practice self-forgiveness and tolerance?

In the holistic world of healing, naturopaths believe that when someone refuses to forgive, let go of a negative situation or resentment, or chooses to live in fear, he or she may face diseases that may cause great harm.

Use this affirmation to start your healing process:

I will begin this day to forgive all and let go of the past. So be it.

Women, the Nurturers

Most women are the nurturers of their world and, therefore, do not usually take the time to create a magical soul moment with themselves. They should nurture and bond with their own bodies, otherwise they leave themselves open to great harm. In order to create this bond, women must first give themselves permission. My mother's family has a long history of cancer. My grandma, Elonra Madry, was briefly married to my grandfather, James P. Madry. After they were married, my grandfather claimed that she had had an affair and took her children from her. According to a relative, losing her children scarred her and her children for life. When I was a small child, she developed colon cancer and died a very unpleasant death. At the age of 5, I walked into her home and smelled the smell of death. I vowed, then and there, not to die like that. It is my belief that her deep regret and inability to forgive manifested itself as cancer deep inside of her and, eventually, took her life. Can you relate? What do you hold on to that is causing you harm?

There are many simple ways to detox your body for emotional, physical, mental, and spiritual healing. The first is to choose to let go of the past hurts. In such a case, it is best to learn the lesson evident from each hurt and allow these lessons to improve your soul connections with others.

The next way to detox is to receive an energy cleansing from a Reki master or massage therapist. These types of cleansings can clear anger, fear, blocked energy, and negative emotions from your cells, organs, and glands, allowing the body to restore and heal itself.

Another form of detox is to practice yoga. My yoga teacher refers to yoga as a "union" of mind, body, and spirit and states that the practice dates back to 200 B.C. This exercise calms the nervous system, and creates a union among the body, soul, and spirit. When you practice yoga in conjunction with meditation, your ability to focus your attention is enhanced and you are able to discipline yourself to not react to others' negative behaviors as quickly as before.

Music is another activity that can become a solace to our inner souls. It refreshes your soul and helps you to heal.

Try each of these tools when attempting to create better soul connections with others. Start a life-review journal to keep track of the events that happen to you. Then, look back and see what activities caused you to act in negative or positive ways. Adjust your life accordingly.

> *"Keep thy heart with all diligence; for out of it are the issues of life."*
>
> *– Proverbs 4:23, KJV*

We are all God's children on this Earth. Why can't we stay in a forgiving poise while dealing with others? Often when an individual gets remarried and things do not work out like he or she desires, the person creates a world full of self-hatred, envy, unhappiness, and disease. The person is unhappy and feels that everyone around him or her should be unhappy as well. In order to keep your blood pure, you need to remove these negative emotions and choose to live a happy life.

Meditation

Dear Reader,

I am going to share here with you a different type of meditation. I feel the need to talk to you. You are my soul mate because you believe in the power of positive thoughts and the ability to correct your life and set it on its destined path. Our voices and hearts have connected. I am reflected in you as you are reflected in me. Can you see yourself in anyone else in your life? If so, they are also your soul mate. Do you like what you see in them? These reflections can be seen within you as well.

When I write to you, I see you sitting in front of me. I see myself delivering knowledge from God. Can you see me writing to you? I see you reading this information in order to gain a spiritual awareness, while your soul is cooking the unknown. All is well within your soul. Know this and be at peace. Amen.

Vibration Cooking

Fresh Juice

<u>Ingredients</u>

A handful of fresh spinach

2 large carrots

3 garlic cloves

½ of a cucumber

3 sticks of celery

1 apple

    Run all of the items through a juicer. Enjoy!

Chapter 6

Why Aren't You Writing?

"One writes to teach, to move or to delight."
– Rodolphus Agricola

Do you have a book that's unwritten within your soul? What's keeping you from writing? When are you going to start your writing process? Do you want to write for your own personal enjoyment or to be published? Some people write to leave a legacy for their children. I write for all three reasons! Are you waiting to be motivated or inspired? Maybe you are afraid that by committing your ideas to paper, others will be able to see the weak areas of your life. Or maybe you are afraid that you will not have enough time to commit to the project. Are you letting your lack of computer skills hold you back? Do you lack confidence in yourself? I did once. Reread the quote above. Why do you write?

Have you had dreams of writing a book? On many occasions, I have dreamt that I was in a corner writing a book. Then, I dreamt that I was holding my last book and shaking all over. I dreamt about the cover of my last book with the title in gold and my name standing out.

I have written four published books in 14 years. God has blessed me with the ability to tap into His Infinite Wisdom in order to write these books. In return, I have trusted the unseen powers of God to help and guide me without question. My inspiration to write comes solely and directly from God. He has also provided others along the way to help me in areas in which I may seek assistance. These individuals help me to reach my ultimate potential.

What's Cooking in Your Soul

Upon writing this book, I placed an ad on Craigslist for assistance and received the help that I needed.

Each book is different and I know that I have had Divine angels assisting me along the way. In order to accept help from the angels and God, you must understand and accept that Divine Guidance is directing and operating your life as you write. If you are one who questions your abilities and lives in a sea of doubt, do not allow these thoughts to cloud your ambitions any longer. In times of doubt, I often turn to Ralph Waldo Trine. His book, *In Tune with the Infinite*, is one that I often find inspiring and helpful.

When one becomes thoroughly individualized, he enters into the realm of all knowledge and wisdom; and to be individualized is to recognize no power outside of the Infinite Power that is back of all. When one recognizes this great fact and opens himself to this Spirit of Infinite Wisdom, he then enters upon the road to the true education, and mysteries that before were closed now reveal themselves to him. This must indeed be the foundation of all true education, this evolving from within, this evolving of what has been involved by the Infinite Power. (1897, p. 100)

If you are afraid that you lack a skill or the education to commit your thoughts to paper, then ask God for help and first write your thoughts in a journal. Doing this action will give you the confidence to begin writing your own book. If you open yourself to the highest wisdom, God will work through you and reveal His words through your hand. The key is to be a willing vessel to be used by God. Learning to surrender is hard, but well worth it in the end!

Parents Are Lifesavers

When my children were in school, I volunteered at my youngest child's school, which was located in the inner city in a drug-infested neighborhood. The children were bussed into the area from their home districts. The principal asked me to be the Parent/Teacher Club President, and having such a leadership position at the school proved to be a joyful, enlightening, and rewarding experience. After my first year, I was nominated for and won a J. C. Penny Leadership Award. Soon after, other local schools began calling for my help and advice. At first, I answered these calls free of charge, but, soon, I realized that my hobby was actually my calling from God, the start to a wonderful career and a unique way to create a life for myself outside of my home. Up until this point, I was known strictly as a stay-at-home mom.

I began writing a handbook for the schools who called for my advice. One day, I attended an open forum featuring the new director of my child's school, the Metropolitan

Nashville Public School System. As he spoke, I wrote down notes and altered his philosophies and insights to fit in my thoughts on how parents should be involved in their children's schools.

He was featured in several of these open forums. At one forum, a parent asked how parents could become involved in the school system. I went to the microphone and explained what I had initiated in regard to parental involvement at my child's school. At the end of the forum, the director came up to me and told me that he enjoyed my comments. I told him that he should offer me a job. His response was that there weren't any jobs available with a job description to fit my qualifications. I said to him, "Dr. Benjamin, you are the school's director. You can create a job for me. Shall I make an appointment to come and see you?" That is how I created the job that I held for four years with the Metropolitan Nashville Public Schools. It should be noted that I created this position without an advanced degree and only the information that I had gathered during my time as a volunteer.

Remember, this new career started with a simple volunteer position and a desire to help others. However, the turning point was when I committed the ideas that God had given me to paper in the form of the handbook for the other schools.

Persistence Pays Off

While in this position, I needed to create a parental consultant brochure to define the mission of my new job. As a parental consultant, I was allowed to attend three conferences a year. At each conference, I collected business cards from those in attendance who worked in education. I went through every address that I had of publishers that specialized in education and sent them a copy of the brochure. One of these publishing companies was Corwin Press. Within three weeks, I received a phone call from the company asking me if I would be interested in developing a handbook on parental involvement for teachers, parent leaders, and administrators. The acquisition editor told me that they usually ask professors to write such books, but they wanted a "parent who had been there" to share her insights instead. After accepting the assignment, I had to write a proposal for the book.

Writing with the Infinite

At this time, in 1994, I did not have a computer nor did I know how to use one. I decided to ask God for help. He led me to a personal editor who I hired to help me clean up and type my writing. You may find similar help in writing magazines, at colleges, or online in such places as

What's Cooking in Your Soul

Craigslist. By trusting in God, I have always been supplied with the help that I needed.

After I wrote the proposal, I received the contract. Next, I turned to my personal editor to help me with the book. I still did not own a computer, so I handwrote the entire book. Once I had finished a chapter, I would mail it to my Corwin Press editor, who would call me after she received it to discuss and revise the contents. After making the necessary changes, she would mail back the manuscript. This process continued for eight months.

Once they reviewed the chapter, Corwin Press would send me their assessment and critique. In such a process, you must always stay open to the views of others, especially those who are professionals in the business. You must trust them and keep your mind open so that you can learn from them. It is important to keep your mind open to constructive criticism, no matter how hard it may be to hear. Do not take any criticism personally. It is merely meant to help you improve.

When the book was completed, the publishing company sent it to a professor in Nashville for review. His response was that my personal story was missing. The editor from Corwin Press then called to tell me that I needed to include my personal story in the book. At first, I was angry because I thought they wanted me to focus on theory. Nevertheless, I did not stay mad for long as I had a job to do.

Being Tapped on the Shoulder

One night as I lay in my bed, I felt someone tap me on my shoulder. I looked around, but no one was there. I heard a voice say, "Get up and write." I got up and handwrote my story for the next 12 hours. When I was done, my hands hurt so bad that I could not use them. I took the new chapter to someone to edit and type. This chapter is now the first chapter in my book *Parents Are Lifesavers* (1996).

People who aspire to write ask me how I am able to find the time and where I get the inspiration. Below is my plan to action.

1. First, ask God for assistance and surrender yourself to that Living, Loving Spirit. I live alone, so my house is quiet. In addition, where I live, very little outside noise exists to disturb me. Before I begin to write, I enter into a moment of silent meditation to help focus my thoughts. I put on soft music and turn off my phone. I fix a cup of tea, light a candle or incense, and begin to work.

2. If writing is important to your soul, then you make the time. Often, I will get up at 3 a.m.

to write as that is when the Spirit calls to me. As I am self-employed, I have more control over when and how often I write rather than someone who works a 9-to-5 job.

3. **My** inspiration comes from God. He provides me with the power necessary to complete each chapter. I also find inspiration in the events that happen around me, as well as from my friends and children. I always carry a pen and paper with me because I never know when the urge to write will strike. You may think this is funny, but I often get my best inspiration while running, sleeping, or in church!

4. **In** order to successfully create a book, you need to formulate a "plan to action." Without such a plan, you'll never accomplish your goals. For example, I wanted this book to be about what's cooking in your soul. Thus, I put my creativity to work and pulled the cooking concept into stories of my life and formed the book that you are reading. Ask God how you can best serve humanity with a book. Then, move forward to create the book. Use the space below to create your plan to action.

_____

_____

5. **M**aybe you want to publish your writings. If so, many options are available to you. You may choose to self-publish. You may search the Internet for self-publishing companies or talk to someone who has already published a book in order to gain knowledge. Go to a public library or bookstore in order to compare and utilize books on how to write and become published. What should you do once you have written your book and become self-published? Read the magazine *Writer's Guide to Publishing*. Resources such as this one are exceptionally important when it comes to learning how to find and hire the right agent and signing with the right publishing company. Pray about your writing and ask God to help you find the right people. Allow yourself to take full ownership of your literary work. Most published authors with major publishing contracts received them with the help of a literary agent. Accept help and support from anyone who you think

can offer sound advice. Think inside and outside the box while writing. Listen to your inner guidance and know your craft. Mine is writing "lessons learned" from my life and the lives of others. My gift to write is best used to inspire, instruct, empower, and heal others' lives. My work is categorized as Christian, Spiritual, Biography, Psychology, Religion, and Nonfiction. You must understand what defines your writing in order to market or connect with the right literary agent. I was blessed in that Corwin Press called on me to develop an educational book on parental involvement. Such instances of luck do not always happen in the publishing world. Sometimes, you have to use persistence to make your own luck.

Facing Internal Limitations

We all face inner limitations; however, it is what we decide to do with those limitations that determine who we are. For example, St. Teresa of Avila (1515-1582) was a mystic and Roman Catholic nun. Her teachings are designed to instruct, inspire, and delight our souls and illuminate our pathways. The bishops to whom she reported noticed that she had a unique relationship with God, one that they admired and respected. Thus, they instructed her to write about this relationship in order to help others in their relationships with God. When assigned this important task, she questioned her capability to undertake it and felt that her lack of formal education and poor health would hinder her in her abilities. She felt that the responsibility should be undertaken by the "learned men" of the church. However, when the clergy of your church request for you to complete a task, you do not turn them down; she wrote down her thoughts. Her writings have inspired people around the world and will continue to do so for years to come. If she had not been able to be humble and accept the gifts provided to her by the Spirit, we would not have these writings today. Are you ready to write now?

St. Teresa has been a guiding force within my life. I first came to know her by reading her stories and understanding the limitations that she faced. Learning of her ability to overcome her limitations has allowed me to search for the strength to overcome my own limitations. In order to overcome our limitations, we must have faith and trust in God. He will put the Law of Attraction (see Chapter 2) into place when the time is right in your life.

What's Your Story?

We all have a story to tell. Our stories help others along their paths. Some of you may have been sexually abused. Others might have been in a failed marriage, sick, or addicted to drugs. We all have a story to tell that can help inspire others. What defines you? Before you begin to write, decide who and what defines who you are. Do you want to write nonfiction or fiction? Are poems or songs the ways by which you desire to express your stories? Do you want to market a recipe book? Do you want to provide stories of healing to others who have experienced the same situations that you have experienced in your life? Once you have decided who and what defines you, be true to your inner voice and allow it to shine through as you write. Give yourself permission to share your story. Stop being afraid of what your family and friends might say.

Meditation

In the silence, I will become still and relaxed. My hands are still. My body is still. My feet are folded into the lotus pose or Indian pose. I will shut my eyes and when I open them, I will see the clouds above through the trees. Everything outside is still. Words will begin floating into my mind and the Spirit will give me the power to write. I am free to write my story. I will not allow any chains or shackles to hold me down. I have unbound myself and am free. So it is.

Vibration Cooking

Apple Butter

<u>Ingredients</u>

12 apples, washed, cored, and peeled

1 pound of cinnamon candy

A handful of fresh mint

Mint favoring

½ a bag of brown sugar

Cloves

Allspice

Cinnamon

Add all ingredients to a pan and fill the pan with water. Place the pan on the stove on medium heat. Or, you can use a crock pot placed on simmer. Let the mixture simmer for 24 hours on the stove or in the crock pot.

After it has simmered, put the mixture in a blender. Blend it on low speed. Once blended, place the mixture back into the crock pot to simmer for two more hours. You may store the completed apple butter in the refrigerator or can it in mason jars.

This butter is good on toast, biscuits, and pancakes.

Chapter 7

Your Project Is Finished, Now What?

"He who does not look ahead remains behind."
– Spanish Proverb

Your book is published, the CD is completed, your ministry is started, the schooling for your new trade is done, your project is over and accomplished. What's cooking for the next move of your new journey to "get the message" out to others and the world? What are your true feelings about self-promotion, branding, career building, and getting your name out? How's your mental attitude about your success, personal branding, social media, direct services, publicity, marketing, and promotion? Are your thoughts based on limiting fear-based beliefs about your circumstances, such as the way you were raised, a lack of talent, money, or the way you think you look? Oh, don't let me forget that you don't know how to use a personal computer, think you have a lack of education, and no so-called opportunities. As you have read my story and the stories about others within this book, you can see that you *can* be successful at marketing your project – and yourself. First, you must align yourself with your Higher Power for a spiritual and personal transformation to accomplish what's needed to get your message out. Please, start right now taking personal responsibility for your mental attitude. Unless you are inspiring and helping another, stop nursing and rehearsing your past! Break yourself free from holding on to that negative and useless energy that causes frustration and a robbing of energy. Learn from your past experiences, but don't become bound by them. Learn the "life lessons" and look *ahead*, as the Spanish proverb states, not behind. "Failure comes to those who indifferently allow themselves to become failure conscious." (Hill, *Think and Grow Rich*, 1995, p. 17)

Affirm right now:

I am no longer bound and shackled to my past story lines, but free to create my future as a new creation.

Questions for You:

- Do you have a strong belief in yourself?
- Can you see the positive in others?
- Can you seize the moment and take opportunities?
- Are you a giver? Or are you a taker?
- Can you reach out to others in a form of Social Media like Twitter or Facebook, etc.?
- Where does your attention and time go: on the solution or the problem?
- To become successful, one must not give up, but practice persistence. Can you do this?
- Do you step up to the plate and take full responsibility for your actions? No blaming or shaming others.

Tapping into Your Resources

John C. Maxwell has said, "Success landmarks are internal, not external. Look for landmarks." How often do we look for success on our outside? We don't even think to look internally; that is the last place we look. Instead, we look to others – who they are and what they are driving. Then we look to see what our peers are wearing. We never stop to think how we feel about moving up the ladder. We as humans just want to keep up with the Joneses. Look within your soul, not outside yourself.

Association with successful people will help you increase your knowledge and promote yourself better. Try joining an organization, club, class, business group, mixers for your niche, Internet group or class, social media venue, or Internet marketing venue that will shed insights on getting your message perfected and out to the public. Ask successful people for advice and help; I do. I joined the National Speaker Association of Tennessee (NSAT), to learn how to improve my speaking and to increase my speaking and book writing business. That's taking action. The National Speakers Association Chapters offer classes once a month to its members and non-members.

"Don't ever admit that the world has not given you an opportunity."

– Napoleon Hill

Marketing and Promotions: What Is It?

My dears, do you know the difference between *marketing* and *promotions?* Are they both the same? No, but they go hand to hand. Are you the service? I am a massage therapist, so my hands are the service. Is there a product that you have developed that is a service or project? Then on the other hand, I create books and my books are products. The online *Encarta Dictionary* describes *marketing* as: "the business activity of presenting products or services in such a way as to make them desirable." As I used Wikipedia, I learned also that *marketing* is "an action of set intentions for creating, delivering, communicating, and selling your products that create customer value." This may also be used for maintaining a satisfied partnership between you and your customers or clients.

Promotions, as defined on Wikipedia, "helps get your message, word, and product out by offering discounts, coupons, or free merchandise to the customers." Stop and think about these two terms and write here what you understand about them:

Marketing: _____

Promotions: _____

How to Do It?

Boy, it's so easy to find the creative time to implement our dreams and bring them to pass. After the dream has been created, the challenge is how to market the product and sell it. Time and again, we don't attempt to market or promote and the project stays on the shelf, in the drawer, in the house, or in the business. Most of us start from the ground floor and work our way up. We become the inventor, creator, the candlestick maker, the advertiser, the shipper, the manager, and the deliverer. That's a big job, but it's your invention and your creation, not someone else's. We are everything. What's cooking with your dreams? Is it now the time for your dreams to become real? There must be a balance.

Take a pause, breathe deeply. Take a healthy dose of fresh air into your lungs slowly. Now, breathe it all out. What you just read may be overwhelming. Affirm:

I can do this next step on my journey. With the Spirit living inside of me and assisting me, I will.

> Right now at this moment, if you have a project finished or you would like to wrap it up, make a commitment to do so. Marketing your project is one of the most important steps after bringing

your project to a close. Are you ready to hear how I market my projects?

What's Cooking?

As you know, this is my fourth book in 14 years. In the case of my first book, I had a contract through Corwin Press Educational Publisher before the content of the book was determined. Long before the book was over, I saw visions of *who* needed my new book and *why*. Then I stopped there and saw educators, administrators, parent leaders, and community leaders that needed the information presented within the book.

The Who

I wrote the vision of my new book and how to market it down on paper. Who is your target? What is your target demographic and age?

The What

The vision of *who, what, how,* and *when*. My plan to action was then to go out in Nashville and across the United States to as many educational conferences and workshops as possible to get business cards and network.

The How

Networking and believing in your dreams, as many of you all ready know, is the key. Most people just want to rely on the Internet alone, but a personal contact by phone and regular mail is still important. Don't underestimate the value of personal contact face to face, though it appears to be a lost art now. As time went by while I was writing, I collected business cards and kept the vision within me of sending out a letter (by regular mail) informing those new contacts about the book once it went to press. That was my marketing plan. I sent about 400 flyers by mail.

The When

I didn't stop after the first year. I still mail out flyers about the book created in 1996, *Parents Are Lifesavers*, even though the publisher was paying for the book and marketing. I assisted my sales because I was letting others know about this new product. A librarian in my city took the information back to a meeting and the Metro Nashville Public Library System ordered my books for all of the libraries.

My marketing plan was so clear to me that I followed and wrote down what I envisioned. This is the *who, what, how, and when* – the four Ws. Remember, I am sharing my experience with my first book, *Parents Are Lifesavers*, which is used in school districts around the world and is currently being reprinted.

I Did Not Stop There

Once the book went live, I ordered $600 worth of books at my discount. Then my next step was my own personal book and self-promotions. I started by calling bookstores in the surrounding area to buy my books from me and let me do a book signing. Often in this process one may have to mail a book out for review. That's called promotions: getting the word out. Most of the time, this will cost you more, especially if you are unknown in the field you are pursuing. But in the long run, it will pay off. To get my name out, I sold books at the bookstore without making a profit. Next, I tried to find a venue that was related to my books, like radio or TV talk show programs that relate to the same topics as my books. Then I looked for publications with a similar interest as well.

Here's another example of promotions. My minister friend created a CD on healing. The church where she pastors has a bookstore and members and visitors buy her product through the store. Once, she held a presentation for her organizational ministers group and sold her CDs following the presentation. Right now she is not marketing the CD outside of her organization.

What Do You Have?

Let's say you have a music or healing CD and you are a pastor of church. Then what? (And, many of you do because you record your messages every Sunday.) What have you done? What are you willing to do? For years artists have sold their projects out of the trunk of their cars. I myself have and still do the same. Many have gigs where they play or perform in night clubs, bars, churches, other events, and special occasions, then following the performance have a table with their materials for sale, including CDs, stickers, t-shirts, DVDs, and more. On that table they have an e-mail list for signing up for their upcoming events. I use a guest book that I bought online. Personally, living in the "Music City" of Nashville, I have noticed that most artists don't know how to market themselves or their projects. Artists are too shy, or don't believe in their artistry, or themselves. In order to produce a project and get it out to the public, one must believe in one's dreams – in one's project.

In Nashville there is a new company called Vision Distribution (www.visiondistribution.com), and for a one-time fee of $45, they will help get your message out to the world via the Internet. It's more than a bookstore. If you type in the word "distribution" on a search engine on

What's Cooking in Your Soul

the Internet, you may find assistance with promotions and marking your projects.

Recently, I took a class at the National Speaker's Association's Winter Conference. I would like to share a part of the class with you right now. The presenter is the Personal Branding Strategist, Speaker, Author, and Coach Lethia Owens. Her belief, which I am convinced is true, is that a person or company must be bold, stand out, and get noticed. I have written many books, and my last two are on Spiritual and Personal Transformation, yet she had to point out to me that night that I didn't have a personal brand. I would like to share a few of my notes, but I would also like for you all to see www.LethiaOwens.com today. After she shared with me that I didn't have a personal brand, I went home and looked on Google for "spiritual and personal transformation" (the niche market for my brand). Guess what, my dears, my site wasn't on the search results for any Internet search engines. Lethia taught us how to make a newsletter and build an irresistible "Personal Brand."

Here are some steps I took towards Personal Branding:

- First, I changed my website to say: "Are you ready for Spiritual and Personal Transformation?"

- Next, I asked my website guy to put me on a search engine under (you got it) Spiritual and Personal Transformation.
- Then I wrote a newsletter for my website titled (you're right again) "Are You Ready for a Spiritual and Personal Transformation?"
- She taught us to post newsletters as an ezine article. I put my newsletter there with my keywords (which you know by now).
- Then she taught us how to convert that newsletter into a .PDF and put in on Scrib.com, then make it into a PowerPoint presentation and upload to Slideshare.net.
- Last, she suggested I make small, two- to three-minute videos to post on youtube.com.

There is much more! Check out this powerful and knowledgeable woman!

"Between saying and doing many a pair of shoes worn out."

– Italian Proverb

The Success Journey

Henry Ford stated, "The whole secret of a successful life is to find out what it is one's destiny to do, and then do it." We create our dreams, we write and sing, see our visions, or paint our creations; some of us hear our projects, and we work hard to pay for the projects. God sends us the right people to assist us; Angels and the Spirit of God guide and direct our path. What, then, are we afraid of?

The Foreword of *The Science of Mind Textbook*, by Dr. Ernest Holmes, states:

I do not claim to have discovered any new Truth. The Truth has been known in every age by a few, but the great mass of people has never dreamed that we live in a mental and spiritual world. Today, however there is a great inquiry into the deeper meaning of life because the race has reached a state of unfoldment where a broader scope is possible. (2007, p. 11)

The Power of a Dream starts with a creative thought, faith, the power of imagination, desire, a vision deep inside of something you were born to do, and a commitment. Dreams can help you: they can give you direction, increase your potential, and help you to grow and develop and seize the moment. One must set their priorities for their hopes and dreams to come to fruition. Are you willing to "let go" of fear? Can you value your dreams and your destiny?

"Fear is nothing more than the negative use of faith."
– Ernest Holmes

Can you stop and ponder these insightful words by Holmes on *Imagination* from the lessons of *The Science of Mind Textbook?*

> Imagination taps the very roots of Being and utilizes the same Power that brought the worlds forth from Chaos. "The worlds were framed by the word of God." Imagination is the power of the word, while will is the directive agency, denoting the purpose for which the word is spoken. Man reproduces the power to create and, in his own life, controls his destiny through the activity of his word. This word cannot be willed, but it can be imagined, or imaged forth, into expression. (2007, p. 126)

More on Book Promotions

First and foremost, is a commitment to your ideas and creative projects. I have been writing this information to you for two days now. Yesterday, I was up at 3 a.m. and I wrote for four hours. Currently, I am awake at 2 a.m. to write. To crawl out of my warm bed and outside is five inches of beautiful white snow – I am dedicated to you, my dear readers, and my work! You are my soul mates. After my meditation and affirmations, I fix a hot cup of herbal tea and soothing music is playing in the background of my office. I ask for Divine guidance from the Spirit to use me as an instrument for this book of inspiration from "life lessons" learned and to help you along your spiritual and personal transformation journey. (Oh, yeah, I bought new incense – I would like to recommend the Forest!)

At this moment, of time, January 31, 2010, I have three finished books (projects). For two years following the birth of my book *In Due Season*, I was unable to market the book the way I knew how. One reason was that the timing was not right, but the knowledge of what to do wasn't there either. Nonetheless, I did the very best I knew to do: workshop, sell, visit a few bookstores across the country, and visit libraries. When I presented a workshop or held a Lifestyle Coaching session, I sold books. Really, I have been in transit for the last two and a half years, living between Nashville, TN and Carrollton, GA. This past September, I paid the small fee to join Vision Distribution. They took my two books, *In Due Season* (2007) and *Poise for the Runway of Your Life* (2009). As previously mentioned, I have authored another book, *Parents Are Lifesavers* (1996); however, Corwin Press Publications owns that book.

Vision Distribution

After becoming distributed by Vision Distribution, the owner shared with me how to create a one-sheet on my books. Corwin Press did this for my first book and mailed me flyers whenever I needed them. Maybe you do not know what a one-sheet is. It is your project and color image on the sheet. Then all the important information, including the ISBN numbers, publisher, name, title, year and date of the project, the author's name, how to buy from what venues and Internet sources, and an overview of the project. Then you add the contact information for the author.

Once this process was completed, Vision Distribution asked me to e-mail this out to college departments that my book might interest. I chose Spirituality and Psychology Departments and my assistant and I researched on where the departments were located. While she sent attachments via e-mail, I sent a hard copy about the books. During this time, *Poise for the Runway of Your Life* was four weeks away from coming live. So you see, I did not wait until the book was ready and published, I went to work four weeks ahead of time. It's been said that "timing is everything," and, my dear readers, it is. Don't get ahead of God and rush. Seek the answers from the Spirit and then wait patiently. After that task, we located Women's Organizations, radio and TV talk shows, and churches, mailing the one-sheets in the same way. Around the New Year, I started calling churches and bookstores to do a follow-up. That process started heavily in January, 2010. I fasted with prayer and focused my attention on marketing and promotions for two months into the New Year.

Which means I have ordered books and mailed them out for promotions. Two weeks after publication of my third book, I sought a metaphysics or New Thought Movement distributor. I found a company called New Leaf and they bought my books. Guess what? I lived in Douglasville, GA for one year after moving from Carrollton, GA. New Leaf Distribution was three miles from my apartment, though at that time I was unaware of how close they were. You see, it's all about the timing. The term *metaphysics*, as defined in *The Ernest Holmes New Thought Dictionary*, is "Viewing the universe as a mental spiritual system, governed by laws of thought. Man, being part of this system, discovers the same laws inherent within his own being and may apply them to definite purpose" (Holmes, 1991, p. 93). The phrase *New Thought Movement*, according to Holmes in the same book, is "the groups, Societies, religious and spiritual organizations built upon the New Thought philosophy, leaving room for ample independent individualism. The principles governing the New Thought Movement are universal but individually and independently applied" (p. 100).

Even when you self-publish, most publishers will link you with all the online booksellers who sell books, such as Amazon, Barnes and Noble, or Borders. After attending the Promotions workshop by "Master Mind" Lethia Owens, I hired a Virtual Assistant (VA) to help me with promoting my personal branding in my work. After the workshop, we worked for three days straight to implement what I learned from that one-and-a-half hour class. Maybe you are like me and not very skilled at the personal computer or Social Networking. I hired her and now it is done. Now we have to update it daily! If you are like me and need assistance so that you can work on other things, look up Callkayla.com.

Meditation

This morning when I look out my office window, I see nature. I welcome God's signs of Winter. Snowy rooftops, icicles on barren tree limbs. Animals search for water and food. I throw out an old piece of chicken and popcorn and the birds love it. The snow is so heavy and crunchy when you walk. Everything in nature is white and bright. This is just a season – everything will change.

Let's pause right now and see this scene. Picture a blanket of white snow all over your city. Time has stopped. People are living in the *Now*! They must deal with this weather now – not tomorrow, but today. Put some soft music on, light some candles, darken your area, and go into a silence of nothing. When the chatter keeps on going in your mind, let it become numb. Then it too will become quiet and still. See nothing but a blanket of white snow, the purest white you can imagine. See the sun beaming light from the heavens, the sky radiating the Earth. Become still and silent. You can do it. Think nothing. Do nothing. Hear nothing. Breathe big breaths of air and let it out from your belly! Think and do nothing.

Now ask the Spirit how you may serve this day. Wait. Be still and do nothing. Sit in a posture of receiving. Then ask for guidance and direction toward your marketing and promotions. Again sit still and do nothing. Open your hands palms up to the sky to be filled from the overflow of the universe. Know that *all* answers and direction will be given unto you according to your belief in the Spirit.

Just like the birds on a snowy day that eat, sing, play, and fly in faith, so can we! So be it!

Vibration Cooking

Real Snow Ice Cream

<u>Ingredients</u>

Bowl fresh snow

Pinch vanilla

Chopped peppermint candy

2 pinches sugar

Semisweet chocolate chips

If there is untouched snow outside, scoop up a bowlful. Then add the vanilla, peppermint candy, and sugar and stir. Put in the freezer for 15-20 minutes. Add semisweet chocolate chips. Then, hurry up and eat it!

Chapter 8

Changing Our Old Patterns of Thinking to Create New Patterns!

"Do not be conformed to this world, but be transformed by the renewal of your mind,
that you may prove what is the will of God, what is good and acceptable and perfect."

– Romans 12:2, KJV

Have you ever had an old pair of tennis shoes that you needed to replace, but did not want to because they were comfortable and fit so well? Instead, you simply kept them, washing them when they became dirty, even though they never really got clean. Eventually, you gave in and purchased a new pair, but still kept the old pair because you just could not bear to part with them.

Just like the old tennis shoes, we sometimes need to replace our old ways of thinking with new ideas. According to *The World Book Complete Word Power Library* (1984), to *transform* means "to change, convert, transmute [or] transfigure" (p. 412). In *Random House Webster's Quotationary*, Kazimierz Dabrowski took this idea one step further and stated that to *transform* is to "replace old values with new ones in the evolution of conscious life" (Frank, 1998, p. 874). Could it be that in our lives we have too many desires and wants toward a transfiguration of our hearts, lives, and souls? Are we too afraid to break free from our old habits and rituals? Why can't we "break free" from the old? Is it because we are too comfortable with what we are still doing or because it fits so well within our lives? Often, the patterns that we create help us to cope with our lives when we face fear. We often use fear to retreat into our comfort zone as we resist change. In order for our *spiritual growth* to transpire, we must be willing to change our patterns. The negative patterns become so

What's Cooking in Your Soul

heavy within our souls that they weigh us down. Release them to God one step at a time and let them float away.

I would like to pose these questions before we go any further: How sacred is the call for transformation in our lives? How does transformation affect our world and our lives?

This sacred transformation is an invitation to our souls for change, a mysterious voice tapping within and tugging on our hearts. It cannot be ignored or denied and contains, by definition, the purest message and a promise of freedom. It touches us at the center of our hearts, souls, and minds. When such a call occurs and we hear it – really hear it – our shift to a higher consciousness is assured. However, most of us run and hide from the opportunity for spiritual growth. As travelers on this Earth, we are here to grow and develop our souls and minds. I have witnessed many kindred spirits who think that they do not need to change, that they are great just as they are. We all have patterns in our lives that we learned in childhood, our teen years, or during adulthood that need to be examined if our patterns are to be redone or replaced.

This past fall, I undertook a personal and business assessment of my life because I learned that I would no longer be able to advertise with a newspaper upon which I had become dependent to generate business. After several days of disarray, I remembered the old adage, "To thy own self be true." After I calmed down, I asked my Higher Self "What must I do?" I asked myself what my intentions were for my life. I decided that it was time to reposition myself. In being true to myself, I allowed myself to feel the negative emotions of fear, worry, and doubt. Then, with confidence, I developed my plan to action. I did not allow myself to remain in the valley of negative emotions. This process may not happen quickly for everyone. For me, the process is quite long as I cannot process my feelings quickly. I undertake the process in my own way and in my own time. In the end, I give myself permission to feel all that I need to feel and move freely through the negative vibrations.

Reposition Yourself

Every morning, my day starts at 4:30 a.m. as I get ready to head to the gym. As I lie in bed, I set my life's intentions by saying my prayers and personal affirmations. These actions help to affirm in my mind and heart that I have an abundance, which is an overflow from the Universe, prosperity of everything that I need on my journey, and that my life will flourish. Then, I continue to say that I have success, happiness, and health in my life. Dear readers, right now, it is 1 a.m. and I am writing to you my thoughts. I have said my affirmations while still and set my intentions on what I want to say to you.

Psalm 46:10-11 (NIV)

Every day as I head to the YMCA to run and walk around the indoor track, my affirmations are reinforced by a scripture written on the wall. Psalm 46:10-11 (NIV) clearly reminds us to:

Be still, [do not move, be quiet, stop talking], and know that I am God; [Who is in control, you or God? It is a time to trust God and no one else.] I will be exalted among the nations; I will be exalted in the earth! The Lord of host is with us; The God of Jacob is our refuge.

As I exercise, I use the time for spiritual practice. Maybe you are not sure what a spiritual practice is. Mine consists of listening to the still, small voice within coupled with meditation, prayer, eating wholesome foods, keeping a journal, attending a center or church, and doing uplifting activities.

This scripture never meant more to me than when I was assessing my new plans for my advertising. My spiritual practice helped me to decide that I must focus not on my woes, but on discovering a way to increase my funds and business without an ad in the local paper.

A dear friend of mine had been mentoring me on how to increase my business and writing career. On the second day of my mentoring, he told me that I should market myself on the Internet. It was then that I realized that he was placed on my path to guide me. Such occurrences have happened in your life as well. Can you recall any? We only need to be humble enough to listen to the advice that these individuals give to us. God puts people into our lives for a reason, a season, or a lifetime. How many of us have been given great advice, but did not listen? Sometimes, we are blinded by our own old ways of thinking, other times by pride or ego. Many of us think that we know more than others and, therefore, do not welcome the help of others. Such actions constitute false pride. Our lives would be better if we would simply adopt an attitude of gratefulness and become humble enough to listen to others. If we are not humble enough to listen to the advice of others, we are only hurting ourselves. Is this fair to the life that God is trying to give us? What do you want to see reflected in your mirror? Is it time to change your pattern?

Becoming My Inner Coach

I thought that that day in the middle of the fall was going to be the end of the world as I knew it…and I was right. It was the beginning of a new world, an opening that I could have never before conceived. I took my mentor's advice and began placing ads on the Internet for my businesses. Often, one website would lead me to another and another and, soon, I had a network of websites on which I could advertise, placing my services in front of

What's Cooking in Your Soul

more people than I could have previously imagined. You know, it has been said that God works in mysterious ways. Who knew that my business would increase by marketing on the Internet? The benefits that I have reaped since advertising on the Internet have deepened my faith and trust in God and myself.

It has been said that, often life's disappointments are God's ways of opening new paths and opportunities to us. Can we trust God's processes? We must be our own "inner coaches" in order to see, feel, know, and taste these opportunities. Once we are able to recognize these opportunities for what they are, we will be able to teach others to see the gifts that God has laid before us. In order to recognize these opportunities, we must be still and listen. It is only by being still that we can listen to the plan provided to us by the Spirit. Once we have received the plan, we must put it into place and exercise our faith. We must not falter from our new path regardless of the distractions that may fall upon us. It is only by following this path and removing our distractions that we will realize God's plan for our lives.

Here is a summary of how I became my "inner coach" and motivated myself to get to where I am today.

1. First, I had to let go of my fear, doubt, and worry and, instead, trust God. Then, with faith, I tapped into the Universal resources

on this Earth. I knew that a perfect plan was waiting for me.

2. Next, I set my intentions on what I wanted to create and what I desired.

3. After my desires were set, I waited in the spirit of expectancy. One must go within for answers and for this action to work, you must become still and quiet. Can you do the same when faced with the unknown? Let go of trying to find out the how and when of a plan and simply wait for God to answer these questions for you. Do you know who your Higher Power is? This opportunity is a chance to examine your beliefs and find out your values. Some people think that their values are connected to their clothing, money, physical possessions, job title, self-importance, and knowledge. Do you know who you are in the image of God? Do you know what it means to be made or created in the image of God? I am not going to put an answer here, as I want you to contemplate what that truth means to you. Who are you without the outside things that you feel define you? As you look within, examine what your soul needs.

What's Cooking in Your Soul

4. **I** meditated upon what I needed to do to increase my income and business. The answer was an increase in volume, activity, and money within the week. At that time, I had to hear my phone ring in order to make appointments for potential customers to come in for massages, be booked for workshops, or sell my books. My desires were for people to want my services and for me to be able to pay my household bills without effort. I knew what I was willing to do in order to achieve the results I desired. I held that potential investment in my mind's eye and gave thanks.

5. **A**fter meditating on these goals, I put a plan into place. I began marketing myself on the Internet for about three hours a day for my books and two hours a day for my massages. Soon, all of my bills were paid on time. I attribute my success to my belief in God. When you meditate, what do you see, hear, or feel? Often, I hear my inner fears and doubts. I allow these fears and doubts to bubble to the surface so that I can combat them with my faith and trust in God. What are the lessons that you have learned from a stressful

situation? These lessons are the messages of life and should be taken to heart.

6. **S**hortly after I put my plan into action, blessings began to occur in my life, simply because I followed my faith in God and in His advice and promptings. Can you listen to others when they, following the promptings of God, try to help you? Examine your heart. See if you are full of pride and closed to the advice of others, and, subsequently, to God, who has sent these individuals to your side.

7. **I** know from my past experiences that when one door closes, God will open another in due time. I simply needed to wait for this door to open and when it did, I began to understand God's plan. My words of comfort to you are to do as told in the book of Isaiah 40:31 (KJV): "But they that wait upon the Lord shall renew their strength, they shall mount up with wings like eagles, they shall run and not be weary, they shall walk and not faint."

8. **O**nce I understood God's plan, I began my new journey. All of the blessings that have come my way have come about because of my faith and trust in God. Becoming your own

inner coach is easy if you simply listen to the Spirit's promptings and then act.
9. **F**inally, I gave thanks to God for the blessings and answers that were coming to me. Stay in a posture of expectancy and gratitude.

Meditation

Put on some soft instrumental music. Look within your soul and see all of your heart's desires. Set your intentions on what you desire. Hold that picture in your mind's eye. You can achieve these desires if only you change your patterns. You may ask how you can change your old patterns when you have become so comfortable within them. The answer may live within someone else. Maybe you need to ask for someone else, such as a lifestyle coach, to look at your life and help you. Regardless, you need to give yourself permission to dream. Without this permission, you will not be able to create the new goals and desires that will allow you to change your old patterns. Look to your dreams to find these goals and desires and then use them to tap into the Mind of God and find your true path. Use this newfound knowledge to change your patterns into ones better suited to achieving your new goals.

Write down a list of the people, places, food, and events that you would like to let go of. Tear this list up. Now, write a list of the things you would like to implement in your life. Look at this new list once a day for 40 days.

If you imagine and look at your goals, you have a better chance of achieving them. I see myself writing my story. I see myself skiing and having fun. I see my love mate and myself at dinner on the ocean front. I see myself shopping. I see myself 30 pounds lighter. I see it. I feel it. I believe it. Amen.

Affirmation

Today, I will look into my heart and soul and see my desires. As I set my intentions, I see, feel, and know that God will bring all to pass. So it is.

Vibration Cooking

Low Sugar Harvest Melt Cookies

<u>Ingredients</u>

1 large sweet potato

2 handfuls of old fashion rolled oatmeal

2 handfuls of whole wheat flour

A pinch of baking soda

A pinch of sea salt

A pinch of cloves

A pinch of allspice

A handful of raisins

A handful of chopped nuts

A handful of brown sugar

A pint of applesauce

Bake the sweet potato. Blend the sweet potato with a handful of brown sugar and the spices. Blend the remaining ingredients into this mixture. Roll the mixture into small balls. Flatten each ball. Place each ball on a cookie sheet. Push your thumb into the middle of each ball. Add strawberry jam in the thumbprint. Cook at 350° for 20 minutes or until the cookies are brown around the edges.

Chapter 9

Train up a Child

*"Let the children come to me, do not hinder them;
for to such belongs the kingdom of God."*

– Mark 10:14, KJV

In Psalms 123:3 (KJV), it is written "Children are a heritage of the Lord, the fruit of the womb, a reward." A "heritage of the Lord," what does that mean to you? Does it reflect that our children are a part of God's image and a major part of His family, like you and me?

When people find out that I have six children, some ask, "Are they all from the same father?" Others ask, "Do you know what caused those six children?" or "Did you dream about or plan those six children?" To these people, I say, "Yes, I have dreamt of my children my entire life." Once, I had a well-meaning family member tell another person that once my husband and I had our twins (children 3 and 4), that we should stop. My response was "Whose business is it?" I believe that it is only the business of God and the parents, as long as the parents are able to provide sufficiently for the family and each child. If you have children, how important are they to you? Are they connected to your Divine heritage?

The Dreams Live On

When I was 12 years old, I dreamed about modeling, working in fashion, and having a large family, in that order. At that time, it was not socially acceptable to have young children after the age of 30. However, it was my desire to have a career in fashion, be a fashion model, and become a published writer before having children. In addition, at this

What's Cooking in Your Soul

time, I did not feel that marriage was important in one's life. Throughout my childhood, I only saw one example of a successful marriage, my aunt and uncle in Texas. I often desired to live with them, but this desire never came to fruition.

After high school, I began attending a fashion school in Nashville. However, at the age of 17, I became pregnant and dropped out. My mother forced me to have an abortion and, as I was under the age of 18, I did not have a choice. Afterward, I was traumatized and felt a deep guilt over the murder of this innocent, unborn child. It was my belief then, as it is now, that all children have a right to life. In addition, I do not subscribe to the notion that children are to be seen and not heard. Nor do I believe that they should remain voiceless in actions that will affect their lives. It is not only the Earthly mother and father who know best for children, but their God in heaven as well.

This event was simply another in the pattern of my life. Throughout my childhood, I felt unnoticed, different, and unloved by the members of my family. It has taken me many years to accept and let go of these patterns so that I could redesign and remake my patterns. The first step in this process is to simply let go and become willing to make the necessary changes. Making changes within your patterns is much like taking an old piece of fabric and making it into something new. There are so many textures, colors, and patterns from which to choose. We simply must find the ones that are right for us. Don't be afraid to face your past experiences head-on and rewrite your life's story. This process will take time as you will need to reflect on the past and understand what has occurred in your life and how it affects you before you can move on. I like to share some of the situations that have occurred in my life because I feel that by sharing my experiences, I may help others. However, others are not always willing to listen to or hear what I have to say. Other times, they misunderstand the purpose of my story. Therefore, if you desire to tell your story, make sure that the person to whom you are speaking has both their ears and heart open to listening and understanding.

A Turn of Events

After the abortion, I did not have anyone to talk to. I felt alone and hurt and ran away to a friend's house. I had hoped to find a place at which I could lay my head and allow my emotions to settle.

The friend with whom I was staying did not have enough money for food. One day, I offered to purchase food for her. She volunteered her mother's boyfriend to drive me to and from the grocery trip. However, instead of taking me to the grocery store, he took me to a motel room where he held a gun to my head and raped me. Already traumatized by the abortion, I did not report the rape to the police.

The next week, as I looked out of the window at the apartment where I was staying, I saw three men push a man and woman into the trunk of a car. I wrote down the license plate number and called 911. My roommate and I also told the apartment manager. He asked us to take a ride with him and, naively, we agreed. He took us to a house, but feeling uncomfortable, we did not stay long. Later, the police traced the car to that home. It turned out that the home belonged to a well-known drug dealer. The couple was later found alive, tied up in the attic. The apartment manager had known about the activities of the drug dealer and had, most likely, meant us harm by taking us to the dealer's home.

A couple of weeks later, the drug dealer came after me. I broke into an apartment, set it on fire, and called 911. My plan was to divert the people after me so that they would not find me. After calling 911, I called my mother and asked her to come get me. She sent my stepfather and uncle. Once the police arrived, they asked my stepfather to hide me for a few weeks to keep me safe. They decided to send me to my cousin's house. Many times since then, I have asked myself how my life might be different if I had never called 911 about the kidnapping. Although, regardless of the problems that it caused in my life, I am glad that God was able to use me to save someone else's life. If we look for the good in every situation, we will find it.

The Drama Continues to Unfold

In the course of four weeks in 1973, I had been forced to have an abortion, been raped at gunpoint, and had witnessed a kidnapping. To top it off, I still did not have anyone to confide in. My mother took me to a mental health clinic, but I was too afraid to talk to anyone about what had been happening. Instead, I turned to God, whom I talked to on a regular basis. I asked him why I had to go through these events. I knew that my choices had lead to all of the events that had transpired. Have you ever had events in your life that you questioned for many years afterward?

The Pages Turn

When I was 19, my biological father died. I had only seen him once in my life. As a result of his death, I began receiving his veteran and social security benefits. These benefits were the first and only thing that I ever received from him. I used the benefits to pursue my fashion degree and move out of my parent's home.

Shortly after moving out, I secured a part-time job. In addition, the apartment that I had located was within

What's Cooking in Your Soul

walking distance of my school. I felt that things were looking up.

While attending school, I met my future husband and the father of my children. He was engaged to be married, but told me that he didn't have a girlfriend. After we had been dating for a while, he left his fiancée and asked me to marry him. After I agreed, we went to my mother's home to tell her and my stepfather about our engagement. Instead of being happy for us, she asked me if my stepfather had gotten me pregnant two years before. I told her no and stated that he had never looked at me in an inappropriate manner.

Within two years of meeting Joe, we were married. Before we were married, we had never discussed our desire to have children or my desire to work outside of the home. Once we were married, he informed me that he wanted to start a family right away and did not want me to work outside of the home. Four years later, we brought home our first child.

The Plot Thickens

As you have already read in Chapter 1, the first child that we brought home was our beautiful adopted daughter, Jai'. Three years after we brought her home, we were still adjusting to having her in our home. However, at that time, I felt a deep desire within my heart to have another child.

I simply felt the child's presence within my soul. It was as if our spirits were communicating. We decided to return to Nashville Human Services and begin the adoption process a second time. Adoption through this agency was free, so even though we had difficulties with them the last time, we decided to work with them again. Shortly after beginning the process, we discovered that I was pregnant. It turned out that my hunch about being ready for another baby was correct, only the way to bring the child into our home had changed.

From the time that Joshua was conceived until his birth, I had many obstacles to overcome. These obstacles created a negative energy around me and darkened my life. This energy continued until it was time for Joshua to be born. After an intense two-day labor, Joshua was born via c-section. Growing up, Joshua was a wonderful child who loved to play sports, especially football, and swim. He was a member of the boy scouts, attended church on a regular basis, and was a joy to raise.

Then, at the age of 12, one of the neighbor children introduced him to drugs. The next eight years were full of trials and tribulations that he would have a difficult time overcoming. He began using drugs regularly, dropped out of school, quit all of his sports activities, attempted suicide, was in and out of rehab, and, for a time, lived on the streets.

What's Cooking in Your Soul

As a parent, we often want to step onto our children's runways and protect them from harm. However, only God can know anyone's true path and step in to give us inner direction.

The book of Matthew 7:7 (KJV) states "Ask and it shall be given, Seek and ye shall find, Knock and the door will be open to you." Often, when in times of strife or tribulation, we do not seek God, who should be our refuge from the storm. Such a situation existed in Joshua's life. He never looked inside to seek God and ask for help. Instead, he simply looked for new and better drugs to keep him locked in his dream state and away from reality. I wondered what was cooking in his soul.

At the age of 15, Joshua was sentenced to three months in a Juvenile Facility. While, as a mother, it broke my heart to see him locked up in an orange jumpsuit, I also believe that this action saved his life. His incarceration helped me to forgive part of my past as well; a female member of the staff at the facility had sexually abused me when I was 5. I forgave her and asked her to keep an eye on my son. Every action in God's plan has a meaning, whether the purpose is clear at that particular moment or not. You never know when your ability to forgive someone in your past might help someone you love.

Can you forgive yourself for harming others and forgive others who may have harmed you? Remember that giving forgiveness is not enough; you must also be willing to ask forgiveness of those whom you have wronged. Many times in my life, I have asked forgiveness of others. You must push away the painful memories so that they do not leave imprints on your soul. Release them and let go. Move forward into your destiny. Close your eyes and repeat this mantra now:

I forgive myself and others. I choose Love. Amen.

Before he began using drugs, Joshua desired to become a Marine. At the age of 14, he joined the Marine ROTC. However, he dropped out a short time later even though we and his instructors begged him not to. It is my belief that children should be allowed to decide what activities they participate in. I did not agree with his choice, but knew that I had to respect it as it was Joshua's decision. It was a decision that he would have to live with, as we all have to live by the decisions we make in our lives. I encourage you to read my third book, *Poise for the Runaway of Your Life*, to discover Joshua's Divine mission. Hopefully, his story will impact your life or help you in a situation with a family member. My son's life is now one of hope, faith, and trust in God that all will be well with his soul.

Joshua's Drug Experience

Joshua's drug use began at age 12 and continued until he was 20. When he was 20, he tried to kill himself after his daughter was born. After entering his fifth rehabilitation center, he began to turn his life around. He realized that he had reasons to live. God had given him his daughter and an opportunity to share his lessons in order to help others in his position.

I believe that God was calling Joshua into a life within the ministry. At this time, I stepped back and told myself, "Carol, let go. Let God clean up Joshua's life." I knew that I was powerless and needed to hand Joshua's life to the all-powerful One. While, as parents, we usually think that we can fix anything, we need to learn that sometimes all we can do is pray, let go, and let God take over.

At the age of 21, when his life began to turn around, Joshua joined the army. I am a firm believer that you are never too old to fulfill your Divine mission in life. If you have a dream and a desire, create a plan to action and fulfill it. Your Destiny is always tapping on your heart strings, telling your soul to act.

Today, Joshua is 26 and a member of the Special Forces in the U.S. Army. He is married and ready to share his story with the world. This morning, January 9, 2010, before I began writing this chapter, he spoke at a local church about his experiences. People brought their children and asked questions. No question was left unanswered. He is fulfilling God's mission for him each and every day.

Can you say the same for yourself? Has God given you a mission to fulfill? Are you on the right runway to fulfill His purpose for you? Can you look within and claim your entitlement? God is tapping on your soul. Take a moment and a deep breath. Ask for His guidance and direction. Can you take the negative experiences of your life and help lift another onto their own personal runway?

On January 19, 2010, my son left for Iraq on a Special Forces mission. I will not be able to see or speak to him for the next seven months. I believe in my heart that God has called upon him to serve on this special mission. After seeing him off and crying for two days because I will not be able to communicate with him by phone, I am good! I must be patient and have faith. I will only be able to contact him via e-mail and regular mail. My daughter Jai' flew in from Chicago to see her brother and siblings prior to Joshua's departure. I am so thankful to all of my children for their constant care for one another. As of January 22, 2010, I had received my second e-mail from him! I am truly blessed!

Today is April 2, 2010. My son has been gone now in Iraq for two and a half months. Every Thursday is his day until he comes back to the USA. I ask people, family, and churches to pray for his protection and guidance. I sit and see him surrounded by God's light and protection.

Our Next Children

After Joshua was born, we decided to become foster parents. We decided to use, once again, Nashville Human Services. Shortly after completing our training, our phone rang. The organization had two children ready to place in our home! At that time, we had two children of our own and I was soon to find out that I was pregnant with twins! Twins! Regardless, we opened our home to the two foster children and they lived with us for two years.

Picture This

My pregnancy with the twins was different than my pregnancy with Joshua. At four months, the babies were so heavy that I could not walk. I was required to be on bed rest for five hours each day. Thankfully, the Mormon Church stepped in and helped our family function until the twins were born. Joe's family even helped with Joshua and Jai' when they could.

After the twins were born via c-section, my doctor asked me if I wanted my tubes tied. I told him, "No." Before the c-section, I had looked at the family picture in our living room of myself, my husband, and our two children. Instead of two children, I saw six children. I had received the message.

In his book, *Conversations with God*, Neale Donald Walsch asks "How does God talk, and to whom?"

I also communicate with thought. Thoughts and feelings are not the same, although they can occur at the same time. In communicating with thought, I often use images and pictures. For this reason, thoughts are more effective than mere words as tools of communication. (1995, pp. 2-3)

I believe that God talks to everyone. However, not everyone listens. Oftentimes, God communicates, not in words, but in feelings and thoughts.

While Joe only wanted two children, I knew that our fate as parents was in the hands of God. Even though I had my hands full as a full-time homemaker, I knew that I would be glad to bring more children into my home if that was what God desired for us to do.

As we waited for additional children to join our family, the twins grew and enjoyed their time with each other and the other children in our home. They enjoyed playing sports and, unlike Jai', were slow learners. Not all children learn alike. Regardless, they seemed to really enjoy school and never got in trouble. As they are identical twins, we could not tell them apart and had to put fingernail polish on one of them in order to do so!

After high school, Jeremy and Jacob chose not to attend college. Today, they are 24, each have little boys, and work full time. They are wonderful parents and husbands. They are still happy, funny, and love tricking people on the phone! I love them!

My children are devoted to their siblings. Jeremy's wife was due to have her baby on January 24, 2010, five days after Joshua was to leave for his mission. Instead, she convinced the doctor to induce her so that Joshua could see his nephew before he left. The baby was born on January 18, 2010.

Jessica, Child Number 5

When the twins were about 7 months old, I went to the doctor and learned that I was pregnant again with a baby girl, Jessica. My pregnancy with her was a breeze and I didn't have any problems. When she was delivered via c-section, the doctor once again asked if I would like to have my tubes tied. Again, I told him, "No." She was tiny when she was born and still is to this day. In spite of her size, she often ran our home and bossed around the boys.

Jessica became interested in dance at an early age and also enjoyed doing hair. When she was in ninth grade, I secured permission for her to attend cosmetology school a year early. However, after beginning her first year, she dropped out because she felt that she lacked talent. Now, however, she is 22 and a hair stylist.

Unlike my other children, Jessica had anger management issues at school. For four years, I received at least two calls a week about her from the school. Often, as parents, we desire more for our children's education than they desire themselves. In this case, I was simply glad that she graduated.

One of the trials that Jessica has faced in her life has been being the victim of a hate crime. Three years ago, some men attacked her and called her names. She called her brothers for help and they were able to fight one off of her. However, the other one ran her over with a car and she suffered substantial injuries to her legs. The men who committed these acts were arrested. We all came together for Jessica.

While she was in high school, my home was one of stress as she had a deep lack of respect for anyone in authority. My divorce during this time, I feel, did not help her anger issues as my children often let me know how they felt about my decision to drastically change their lives.

In addition, I was dealing daily with fibromyalgia and a host of allergies.

All of these negative vibrations were coupled with the negative vibrations that I was getting from their father.

During this time, he had begun hitting Jessica and later hit Joel, of whom he lost custody for six months. I did not want to have their father arrested, but felt that my children needed to see me protecting them in every way. Therefore, I took the money that I was going to pay on my mortgage and used it to pay for an attorney. I gave my house back to the bank and moved my four children into a two-bedroom apartment.

It is my belief that parents should show love and respect to each other while their children are growing up. A father should not disrespect his children's mother or raise his voice to her in front of the children. A mother, in turn, should respect and honor her children's father. In addition, she should show softness and be able to defend the rights of the children in order to let them be who God intended them to be. However, a mother should not overrule the father in order to achieve this goal.

Children become confused as to their roles in life and the roles of their parents if abuse is present. In the case of my family, I could not stand by and be the soft person. Instead, I needed to protect my family. I hope that my children understand why I did what I did and forgive me. I know that I have forgiven myself.

Today, Jessica has her own apartment and is an assistant manager at a retail service station. She plans to go to college to become a nurse. I think she will be a great nurse as she is compassionate and always thinks of others first.

Joel Communicates, "I Am Baby Number 6."

Being the dreamer that I am, I dreamt of my next baby before I knew he was going to exist. One night, I dreamt that he appeared to me and said, "Don't forget me. I am Joel." Shortly after this dream, I found out that I was pregnant again. This pregnancy was another easy pregnancy that ended in a c-section. After the delivery, the doctor told me that I would not be able to carry any other children. Joel looked like my father, Fred Johnson. When I looked at his soul, I felt that he had an old soul in a baby's body.

One day when he was two, he began to tell me what route to take while I was driving. Then, I began working with him on reading and recognizing things while I was driving. At the age of 3, I had him tested at the Metro Nashville Public Schools Gifted Pre-School Program. He passed with flying colors in Science and Math and started attending the program one day a week. He continued in the gifted program once he started elementary school. However, at age 11, right before I filed for divorce, he dropped out of the gifted program. His decision to drop out was not unexpected as all of my children were experiencing tremendous amounts of trauma and anger at the dissolution of what they perceived to be a happy home. Despite their reactions, I knew that the decision that I was making was the correct one because I had a plan to action in place.

When Joel entered middle school, he started acting out and getting suspended. I began to dread answering the phone. I asked him to attend anger management classes, but he refused. His father and I took him to counseling, but it did not help.

His anger issues continued. Then, two months before he was to graduate high school, he was caught selling drugs and expelled from public school. When he got home, he cried for about 12 hours, fearing that his life and educational plans were over. It was then that we enrolled him in the alternative school across town.

Joel's Words

Below is a mixture of Joel's words on his life and my thoughts on that matter.

"After being expelled for selling drugs that I did not use, I thought my life was over. However, it turned out that this moment was simply my turning point. My brother, Joshua, cried when I told him about the expulsion because he thought that I was going to turn out to be a drug addict like he was, but I wasn't in it to use the drugs. I was in it to make money.

When I arrived at the alternative school, I told my dad that I was out of place. I didn't belong there. I wasn't in a gang. I didn't do drugs or drink alcohol. I just went down the wrong path. I never tried to have bad behavior in high school. The teachers just expected it from me and, therefore, were looking for reasons to bust me. I didn't have a role model to show me how to do things correctly. No one was there to help me define my dreams and goals."

You might be thinking, "Where were Joel's parents?" I did the very best that I could based on my knowledge at the time. In the end, it turned out that Joel didn't need my help to make him into a man; he needed a male role model. He needed his father. During the many times when I had to call the police to my home because of Joel, they would have me call his father. They would tell him that Joel needed a man in his life to take care of him and show him how to be a man.

Today, Joel is in his third year in college and working part-time selling cars. He's quite the businessman.

Looking Back

Parenting is a long-time commitment that requires a large amount of problem solving. Children need to be taught responsibility and accountability while still young. Even the best families and parents make mistakes. As parents, we do not have all of the tools, skills, and answers to help our troubled children. We can take our children to church or centers for religious worship. We can place them in all types of positive activities, but we cannot force them to stay involved. All we can do is try to teach them that they were made in God's image and, therefore, should try to do their best. I tried my best with my children and I think that, now, it shows.

While going through these tough years, it was challenging to hold on to my faith. I had stopped going to church and reading spiritual materials. I was eating everything without any regard to its health value. I gained 43 pounds. I began to drink in order to numb my own inner pain. I was sick and tired of the stress brought into my house by my own children.

One day, I decided to change. I joined the YMCA and began exercising again. I reduced the stress in my life by sending my 14-year-old son, Joel, to live with his father. Jessica, the only other child still at home, was a junior in high school. I decided to reclaim my life and decided that if I didn't like the life that I was reclaiming, then I would create a new one!

Mom's Time

I remembered my childhood dream and began focusing on my goal to model and write books. By the time that I was ready to begin actively pursuing these dreams, Jessica had graduated from high school and I no longer had any children living at home.

While attending modeling school at the age of 50, I had self-esteem issues and, therefore, had problems walking down the runway. I did not feel that I was good enough or smart enough to have everyone look at me. All I could hear were my mother's negative words ringing in my ears. I wrote my mother a letter explaining to her that my stepfather had not gotten me pregnant when I was 17. I mailed this letter to her, hoping for some sort of closure, acknowledgement, or acceptance. However, she never responded or admitted that she had read the letter. Instead, she told my sister that I was mad at her and that she had not made those accusations.

You may wonder why this information is in a chapter about raising children. It is because I feel that the two items are greatly connected. As parents, we will let our children down, just as our children will disappoint us. In the end, we must learn to accept these failures and accept when we are told that we have failed someone else. My children have told me where they thought I failed them. I did not defend myself, instead, I simply let them talk and share. I listened to their reasons and saw their insights. Listening to their views of the situations that we lived through has increased my ability to accept and acknowledge the past. It

What's Cooking in Your Soul

has helped me to grow. God knows that I did my best with what was given to me.

Their ability to tell me where they think I have failed them has allowed me the courage to let Joshua, Jessica, and Joel take full responsibility for their actions and mishaps. Each of them now talks to at-risk youth in hopes of helping others in similar situations. Regardless of any failures on either part, I love my children and they love me. We understand that only by telling the complete truth and being honest with each other can we have the best relationship possible and walk down our personal runways. I am so grateful to God for their love of each other.

I would like you to write down what you desire to let go of in order to move forward on your personal runway:

_____
_____
_____
_____
_____
_____
_____
_____
_____

So be it.

Affirmation

I will let go of the past and understand why it came to be. I am so glad that I can re-create my stories and give them new endings. Thank you, God! So be it.

Meditation

What's cooking in your soul? Do you have children that you need to shape? Make yourself comfortable and sit in a position in which you feel safe. Think when you were pregnant. How did you feel? Your children are born. What a happy day! What's cooking in your soul? They start preschool and then continue through their educational career. What glorious days! Things are changing at home. The mother is crying and the father is drinking. The mother or father stops coming home. The lights have been shut off. No food is on the table. The children do not understand what is going on. The happy feelings have left the house. This is life. What's cooking in your home?

The children begin to act out in school and at home. They are older now and begin hitting or cursing at you. Where did the happy feelings go? This is life. What's cooking in your home?

Changes are not fun when abuse is involved. The children get hit. Mom gets arrested and loses custody.

What's Cooking in Your Soul

What happened to the happy feelings? This is life. What's cooking in your home?

Remember, children are a product of their environment.

Stop! Remember the happy feelings that you had on the day that your children were born. Hold on to those feelings. Move them from the crown of your head, through your spine, down to the pit of your stomach, to your knees and down to the ground through your feet. Let your entire body experience the happy feelings. What's cooking in your soul?

Your child in middle school is now acting out because of the behaviors that he has seen at home. He curses at his math teacher and the principal. You ask, "Where has he learned this behavior?" As you are trying to answer that question, you argue with and curse at your husband in front of your child. How quickly he mirrors the act. What if you showed love to your husband in front of the children? The next day, he would mirror this act and be kind to his math teacher.

Your oldest child gets arrested at 16 for stealing a car. Before you react, stop and remember how happy you were on the day he was born. It is sad how quickly we forget the happy feelings. We only hold on to the angry feelings. This beautiful child has been placed in your care by God. Go to your secret place within your soul. Control your anger and ask God for guidance and direction. Stop! Listen to the voice speaking to you from within. It says, "Be still and know that I am God," (Psalms 46: 10, KJV). Do not move, talk, or make any action. God will take care of the situation. Put your faith and trust in Him.

Parenting is one of the most rewarding and challenging jobs on this Earth. However, with God's guidance and assistance, Divine answers are there to help you along your runway. To hear them, you must become still and understand who is in control. Neither you nor your child is in control. Only God is in control.

When times become stressful, I recommend taking a warm bath with lavender oil and drinking relaxing or bedtime tea. If you must eat, drink a protein smoothie.

Vibration Cooking

High Protein Blueberry Smoothie

I suggest you buy a protein powder from the grocery store before beginning this recipe.

Ingredients

A handful of blueberries

½ cup of bananas

2 scoops protein power

2 cups of blueberry juice

1 peeled orange

A small carton of plain yogurt

12 pieces of crushed ice

Blend all of the ingredients together and drink! Enjoy!

Chapter 10

Exercising Your Rights!

"An early morning walk is a blessing for the whole day."
― *Henry David Thoreau*

Thirteen years ago, I was in a car accident in which I received a bulged disc and damage to the soft tissue in my neck. Shortly thereafter, I was also diagnosed with an auto-immune disorder called fibromyalgia. My neurologist gave me pain and anti-inflammatory medicines. These medicines did not work because I was having sciatic pain. This type of pain is very hard to describe. The closest that I can come is to say that it is like childbirth, very painful. Finally, the doctor was able to give me some medicine that fought the pain, calmed my nerves, and curved my depression: Prozac! Then, he ordered me to go to physical therapy twice a week and walk in a swimming pool. Unfortunately, the medicine caused me to crave sweets and breads, which I ate in large quantities.

The Start of Natural Therapies

One day, after I became tired of still being sick, I remembered the Biblical text in Luke: "Physician, heal thyself" (Luke 4:23, KJV). My mind went back to 14 years earlier when I was 26 and my food was my medicine. I realized that I had forgotten my natural food and herbal path. The natural path for healing is not God's only way for healing, but it has worked for me. I have studied the use of herbal medicines for many years and even attended herbal schools in the United States. I also worked with a nutritionist in my area and drank freshly squeezed vegetable juice long before either was popular. I decided that it was time for me to take personal responsibility for my well-being and seek an alternative healing method. Remember, if you are under a doctor's care, do not stop anything that he is prescribing without first consulting with him.

Rehabilitation without Drugs or Surgery

I sought out a reflexologist to work on the nerve endings of my feet. In the book of Isaiah, he writes "How beautiful upon the mountains are the feet of him that bringeth good tidings" (Isaiah 52:7, KJV). Eunice D. Ingham, in her book, *Stories the Feet Can Tell Thru Reflexology* (1984), describes Reflexology as a science that deals with the principle that there are reflexes in the feet relative to each and every organ and all parts of the body. Stimulating these reflexes properly can help many health problems in a natural way. Following my accident, my back and neck were the major sources of discomfort for me.

Reflexology works by stimulating one or many of the 7,200 nerve endings located in each foot in order to increase fresh blood flow to a particular area of the body. The fresh blood flow removes the tiny crystals in the blood that are causing circulation problems. In particular, I had the reflexologist focus on stimulating my sciatic nerves.

This type of stimulation would allow the crystals to be processed by my kidneys and exit my body in my urine.

Often when I went to his office for my appointment, I would not be able to put pressure on my foot. However, when the therapy session was over, even though there would be pain in my foot, I would be able to walk normally. He recommended that I take calcium and magnesium for my muscles and bones; Vitamin B for my stress; yucca, which is an herbal plant and steroid, for my pain; Omega-3 for my bones and heart; Glucosamine HCI, Chondroitn, Sulfate, and Vitamin C for my joints; skullcap, which is an herb, to help me sleep; and St. John's Wort, an herbal plant, for my depression and pain.

As my energy was very low, I also started drinking fresh juice once again. My daily six-ounce drink consisted of carrots, celery, garlic, cucumber, and spinach.

Two months into my reflexology therapy, I began to visualize, with the help of my reflexologist, my spine healing. He told me to not focus on my pain, but instead to see myself healed and all of my organs functioning properly. I didn't understand the process, but I did it anyway. There is an old saying that sometimes you have to trust in another's words before you can believe in them.

Next, he told me that it was time for me to get massages and go to trigger point therapy. He said that these would

What's Cooking in Your Soul

help with the back and sciatic nerve pain that I had been experiencing as they would relax my soft tissues. I agreed as all I wanted was relief from the discomfort.

My massage therapist used a "deep tissue" process to relieve the tightness in my muscles and used his elbows on my gluteus area to release the pressure on my sciatic nerve. As he did these actions, I could feel the tension leaving my body.

I decided to join the YMCA in order to work on my physical therapy. I participated in water aerobics and used the whirlpool and sauna. Later, after I was given approval by my therapist, I began attending a bicycle class and yoga. When you have major joint challenges and fibromyalgia, you are advised by health professionals to not participate in high impact aerobics, but activities such as water aerobics, bicycles, walking, stretching, and yoga are considered safe activities because they are low impact.

I received my massages once a week and went to the gym three times a week. I had to pay for these services myself, but I considered it an investment. As my marriage was ending, I wondered what I could do to support myself and my children. One day, as I was receiving a massage, I thought, I can do massage therapy and reflexology. It's amazing how one experience can change your life in such a dramatic way. If I had never been in the car wreck, I would never have learned how to help others in the way that I do now. Everything in our lives happens for a reason.

When I began taking my classes to start my new career, I told the director about my back and he recommended that I start a yoga class for back care, which I did. At that time, I was still taking my supplements and taking two back yoga classes a week. I was determined to do bodywork, which includes teaching others how to exercise as well as providing facials, massage therapy, and reflexology, for a living, so I set my goals on creating a speedy recovery and healing process for my body. However, at that time, I didn't know that in order to achieve this goal, I would need to heal mentally, emotionally, and physically. Such healing was easier said than done as my ex-husband was being emotionally abusive to me at the time. This time in my life was very trying and stressful.

It was during this time that I decided that I had to end my marriage, although I feared his reaction to my decision. I knew that I had to make a life and career for myself before I acted so that I would not be left without the ability to support myself and my children. I sought inner healing, knowledge, and education so that I could make a living and be productive in the world. I was channeling my frustrations into exercise, which was helping me to become stronger, ready to begin my new life.

Moving Forward into the Unknown

What's Cooking in Your Soul

After nine months of massage school, I ended my marriage in order to move forward into my destiny of the unknown. Have you ever feared the unknown so much that you did not want to move forward? We wear so many masks in our daily lives that we are often not honest, even with ourselves, in our innermost secret dialogue. I admit, I was fearful and doubted myself, so I put on a mask of being calm and together. Refusing to acknowledge the truth and putting on masks often complicates the situation and causes us increased stress.

My stress was too much for me to bear and I stopped going to my place of worship. I stepped back from God and stopped communicating with the Spirit. However, the Spirit never left me. I ate all the wrong things for my body, mind, and spirit and gained weight. Sugar became a dear friend to me and I focused only on the negative aspects of my home and life. My children were acting out and getting in trouble both at home and at school. I lost my confidence in my ability to make a living doing massages. As my self-confidence dropped, I felt that I would not be able to accomplish my goal of becoming a massage therapist for individuals within the music industry in Nashville, where I live. I felt that they would not hire me because I am black. Boy, was I wrong!

We often set self-imposed limitations on ourselves out of fears that stem from negative emotions that exist within our lives. We must battle against these limitations every day. In order to battle against these emotions, we must arm ourselves with the inner tools necessary, such as a spiritual practice and the knowledge that no limitations exist when you walk with God. Winning such battles is the only way to reach our Divine destinies.

One of my favorite quotes can be found on the wall at the YMCA where I workout: "The only limitations that you will ever have in life are the ones you accept, whether from other people or yourself" (credited to Shayne Baadra).

The first step to winning is to take personal responsibility for your inner conflicts and self-imposed limitations. You can increase your ability to heal by implementing a "spiritual practice," which has been discussed in previous chapters in this book.

However, you may want to:

- Consider or create a new affirmation for yourself
- Design a new spiritual practice
- Locate and attend a center for worship
- Eat wholesome foods
- Meditate
- Pray
- Listen to uplifting music and television programs
- Read inspirational books

What's Cooking in Your Soul

- Exercise
- Practice the art of forgiveness
- Be true to yourself by surrendering to God and your God-self

Are you ready to move forward toward your destiny? What's keeping you back? Are your inner thoughts holding you back?

Create an affirmation here for yourself: _____

_____

_____

_____

_____

_____

So be it!

Do you have a spiritual practice? If not, create one here:

_____

_____

_____

_____

_____

_____

_____

_____

_____

In my mind, I had to change my inner thoughts and set my mind on going further down the path that I wanted to create. I mentioned in the previous chapter that I desired to reclaim my life. I started to do so when I decided to rejoin the gym and take my exercise one day at a time. Due to my muscle pain, I had to start slow with yoga and kickboxing. After each session, I would return home to sit in a bath solution of sea salt, baking soda, Epsom salt, and essential oil of lavender. This solution allowed my muscles to relax as I drank a detoxifying tea. The tea allowed my kidneys and liver to purge themselves of toxins. In addition, I also changed my diet from high carb to low carb and removed beef, pork, and sugar as well. I began drinking lots of herbal tea and at least 9 eight-ounce glasses of water a day. While I do not recommend this exact amount to you, it worked well for my body.

Back on Track

After I had followed the above regimen for six months, I began to add other exercise into my routine. I added Pilates in order to rebuild my abdomen muscles, and another day of kickboxing to increase my weight loss. I had already lost 15 pounds and loved the results of looking skinner and feeling healthier. In addition, I reduced my alcohol consumption to only three glasses of red wine a week and one low carb beer. I was very proud of this accomplishment.

Remembering My Childhood Dreams

You might be asking what exercising has to do with your dreams. Well, as you already know, when I was 12, I wanted to model and work in fashion. After raising six children and being married for half of my life, I had forgotten my inner desires and personal dreams. My destiny! I began to think that I was too old to recapture my dreams, so I suppressed them in my inner soul. This suppression caused my fibromyalgia and other diseases. Then, one day, I saw on television that a local modeling contest was being held for women over 40. At that moment, it was as if I had woken from a long sleep and stepped into my own reality. Going to the gym suddenly took on a whole new purpose and meaning to me. Now, I could not wait to get up and head out the door to my exercise session. It is my belief that our Spirit consists of our body, mind, and soul. All three must be fed and in order physically, mentally, emotionally, and socially, to allow us to perform our daily tasks free from fear, doubt, and worry.

When I took control of my life, I regained my self-confidence. My goal was to become a lifestyle model at age 51. During my journey to this goal, I lost 43 pounds. I went from a size 14 to a size 4. Today, I am a healthy size, between a six and an eight. After two years of implementing my plan to action, I received a modeling contract with Elite of Atlanta and Sharon Smith Talent in Nashville.

By 4:45 a.m. each morning, I have said my personal affirmation ("I have prosperity, abundance, happiness, health, and success in my life. Thank you, God!") and left my house on the way to the gym. Every morning, I drink fresh vegetable juice and a blend of herbal teas. My midmorning breakfast consists of nuts, real butter, cinnamon, oatmeal, and two turkey sausages. I use raw honey for my sweeter. My healthy lifestyle diet consists of low sugar, soy products, popcorn for snacks, fat-free turkey, fish, or chicken, lots of vegetables, and whole grains. I do not eat bread or white potatoes. When I was raising my children, I forced them to eat this way as well and they hated it! They could not wait to go to a friend's house to eat because they "ate like regular people." Nonetheless, not a week goes by that one of my children does not call me to ask me a question about eating healthy or using a holistic remedy. It's amazing how my influence has touched my children.

Meditation

Instead of burning candles, place a pot of water on the stove and bring it to a boil. Place ginger, allspice, cloves, and cinnamon within the pot. Let it simmer on low for a few minutes and then turn it off. It will fill your house with a beautiful, soothing aroma. Give yourself permission to let go of what you have been taught in the past about body image, wholesome eating, vitamins, minerals, and taking care of yourself. Many people often say that they do not have the time or money to spend on having a massage or shopping at a health food store. Can you *not* take the time to invest in yourself? If you don't, then who will?

Repeat the following affirmation:

I give myself permission to be good to myself this day and from now on. I see myself on the massage table next to the beach and hear the beautiful music of the ocean. The sky is light blue and the sun is beaming bright. The mountains are so close that I can see the tops. The therapist rubs long strokes over my back, removing the negative emotions and toxins. She takes peppermint oil and applies it to my temples in order to relax me. Now, she is massaging my hands, bending them back and forth before pulling each finger. She moves to my feet to perform reflexology and I feel it within each organ of my body. My entire body is relaxed and renewed. She finishes with strokes like a feather all over my body and allows me to lie in the sun, feeling the wind and smelling the warm ocean breeze. She recommends I sit in a bath filled with water, sea salt, Epsom salt, baking soda, and lavender oil to further relax.

Can you smell it? Are you relaxed? Allow every bit of fear, doubt, and worry about exercising and treating your body right to melt away. Allow it to float into the clear blue sky. Feel your body become new and revived. Your spirit is lighter because you are now carrying less baggage.

Repeat this exercise regularly in order to shed more baggage and allow yourself a lighter journey down your runway. Say "Yes!" to becoming a new you!

Affirmation

I give myself permission to complete my spiritual practices and bodywork this day!

If you cannot afford or don't have the time to go the gym, check out your cable network. I exercise along with programs on DVDs, Exercise TV, and Fit TV.

Vibration Cooking

Low Sugar Oatmeal Thumbprint Cookies

Do you like cookies? I do and I love the smell as they bake in the oven.

Ingredients

1 handful of whole wheat flour

1 handful of unbleached white flour

1 handful of rolled oatmeal

A pinch of allspice

A pinch of cloves

2 pinches of cinnamon

1 medium-sized sweet potato

1 pint jar of unsweetened applesauce

2 handfuls of raisins

2 handfuls of walnuts

Bake and peel the sweet potato. Mash it.

Preset oven for 350°.

Mix the above ingredients with a hand mixer. Make small balls and then flatten them on an ungreased cookie sheet. Bake for 20 minutes or until brown.

Chapter 11

What Have You Been Cooking in Your Life?

"What's cooking in your soul? Are there dreams and destinies to unfold?"

– Carol S. Batey

As I write this chapter, 2009 is ending. As I reflect on this time last year, I lived in Georgia where I resided for two years while commuting to work in Tennessee. Where were you living? What were you doing? While living in Georgia, and out of my comfort zone, I learned how to deepen my relationship with and give my all to the Spirit. One way that my relationship has deepened with the Spirit was by learning to trust in the Spirit's guidance. When I moved to Georgia, I did not know anyone and sold everything that I owned to pursue my dreams of modeling and writing books. I call this period in my life my period in the wilderness. The only difference is that instead of sleeping in a tent like Father Abraham, I slept in a four bedroom home owned by my cousin.

When I arrived in Georgia, several students who were also living in the home had caused severe damage to it. They put holes the size of grapefruits in the walls, left trash everywhere, smashed a car into the wall of the garage, stained the carpets, and removed the outside deadbolt. I could have fled the home in fear of the unknown, but I stayed and reclaimed it from the students. As I reconstructed his home, my cousin placed money into my account in order to cover my daily expenses and the cost of the reconstruction.

I finished repairing the house on July 3, 2007 and began to ponder what to do with my life. The little town

What's Cooking in Your Soul

in which I lived had a library, so I decided to seek out spiritual books for guidance.

In addition, I decided to write a monthly newsletter for my website. As I conducted the research for these newsletters, I found out that spiritual matters were closest to my heart. As I did not have a job and was quite bored, I decided the best way to fill my time was to contemplate and meditate on the Spirit. My meditation was assisted by the fact that the town was located in a remote country setting complete with a chorus of birds and tall trees.

Before I knew it, I was booked for two workshops presenting "Your Destiny Awaits You;" one at the Phoenix and the Dragon, a local bookstore, in August of 2007 and the other at my church in December of that year. Then, I was booked for the same workshop at the Center for Spiritual Living in West, Georgia in March of 2008, as well as for several book signings!

On Mother's Day of that year, I was invited to present a workshop at a homeless shelter in Georgia, giving inspiration to those who needed to "Hold On To Your Dreams."

On August 23, 2008, I completed my first modeling job for Elite Modeling Agency. I was proud that I had only been in Georgia for one year and had already landed my first paying modeling job. Our timing is not God's timing and all things happen in due season.

On September 15, 2008, I dreamt that I went to a book signing. At the signing, a lady bought a thick book for me to sign. At first, I did not recognize the book as one of mine, as I had only previously written short manuscripts. However, when she handed me the book, I saw my name on the cover and was in shock. When I awoke, I decided that it was time to start on my next book.

After pondering ideas for the book, I decided that the best way to start would be to gather my newsletters into one place and go from there. Then, on November 26, 2008, I flew to Chicago to see my daughter and her boyfriend's family. His mother, the Reverend Alice J. Brown, a minister in East Cleveland, Ohio, and I have become great friends. That weekend, she asked me to conduct a workshop at her church, to which I agreed. We drove from Chicago to East Cleveland and back so that I could fly home on time. The message of the workshop was "Your Destiny Awaits You." The workshop was well received and an awakening for both the attendees and me as many of the people at the event wanted to step into their Divine destinies, but were not ready. I thank God for all of my experiences, regardless of how painful or joyful they have been, because they have brought me to this point in my life. We are on Earth to grow, heal, be inspired, and help others. I write about "life lessons learned" so that others may identify with my life, struggles, and accomplishments. From that moment in East Cleveland, things in my life seemed to move very quickly. During Christmas, I went home to Nashville to visit my family. When I returned to my apartment in Georgia after Christmas, I began to write my third book, *Poise for the Runway of Your Life*. By the start of 2009, I had become fully engrossed in the book.

Then, in February, a local realtor board in West, Georgia booked me to present a workshop. In March, I presented "Your Thoughts Create Your Destiny" at my church in Georgia. It was then that I decided it was time to move back to Nashville as my book was almost complete. When I made my decision, I did not know where I was going to live. The next day, however, I received a phone call from my tax accountant, offering me a home to rent that was within a price range that I could afford.

A few days later, Elite Modeling Agency called to let me know that I had been booked for a commercial. In April of 2009, when I moved back to Nashville, a local paper wrote an article about my personal growth and a Christian radio station interviewed me. Two weeks later, the station called again, this time to ask me to find a sponsor so that I could have a 30-minute talk show. I found a sponsor and was the host for two and a half months, until the funding ran out. On May 9, 2009, I presented "Your Thoughts

Create Your Destiny" at the Living Truth Center in East Cleveland, Ohio. The following day, I was their Mother's Day speaker, presenting "The Power of a Woman."

On May 12, 2009, I began looking for furniture for my new apartment. As I had been transient for the last two years, I did not have a lot of furniture of my own. Thankfully, I had made enough money that I was able to purchase the pieces that I wanted completely in cash. From May until September, I spent the majority of my time focused on creating a home for myself, hosting my radio program, and finishing my book.

At the beginning of August 2009, I entered into the final process necessary to complete my third book, which focused on how to maintain one's balance or poise in life. Then, on September 4, 2009, I was finally ready and submitted my book to several self-publishing printers.

Relationships and Partnerships

From September 2008 to September 2009, I dated a man who taught me valuable lessons about who I am in a relationship. After the relationship ended, I learned that I am a giver who often sees past another's shortcomings. I also learned that I love to create a partnership with the right man. Unfortunately, these partnerships do not always end up being 50/50. This relationship reminded me that I need to remain true to myself regardless of what my partner does in his life and in our relationship. One must live life without regrets. In order to move forward, you need to be able to grow and learn from the trials and tribulations that you encounter.

In October of 2009, I met a different businessman who I dated for three and a half months. He was the first man in 11 years with whom I thought I had a true connection. He gave me advice, provided copies for my readers while I worked on the book, and helped me monetarily without me having to ask.

Then, suddenly, our relationship started to die. First, our communication decreased and changed and then he did not have enough time to spend with me because of his business. It was time for the relationship to end. Did that decision cause me pain? Yes, I cried for several days. Nonetheless, it was the right choice. Now, I am able to envision the right person for me, as he will have many of the same qualities that I admired in this man.

Five weeks after the end of this relationship, I regrouped and decided to use the "Law of Attraction" in order to re-create the life that I wanted.

Today, I live in Tennessee near my son who is in the Special Forces. Chapter 11 of my previous book, *Poise for the Runway of Your Life* (2009), and Chapter 9 in this book focus on his life. Regardless of where he has been stationed, I have always lived within five hours or less of his location. My location in relation to him has always been a blessing, as I have often been able to bring his daughter to him for visits, which has not only benefitted him and his daughter, but allowed me to have precious time with my granddaughter that I might not have otherwise had.

On November 7, 2009, he and I spoke on a radio talk show about his past drug usage and how his personal relationship with his Sacred Source has helped him to kick his eight-year habit. Recently, he has begun speaking to youth at a local church about his past in order to help lead them down the correct runway.

Who Is Your Sacred Source?

At this point, I would like to ask you how you feel about your relationship with the Spirit or your Sacred Source. A few holy names for your Higher Power might be Jesus Christ, God the Father, Saint, Buddha, Allah, Deity, or Krishna. Many people attend church or a religious center and do not have a personal relationship with a Higher Power. Often, we feel and see our connection with our Higher Power through another man, woman, or child that has come into our life. While these occurrences are Holy and magical moments, for me there is only one source, God.

Mirror, Mirror on the Wall

Think of the Michael Jackson song, *Man in the Mirror*. This song talks about how you are the only person who can change your life. Do you have the inner courage to change your patterns? Are you ready to change? Can you look within your soul and see its needs? What would your soul tell you if it could talk? Do you pay attention when your soul is trying to tell you something? Often, we are too busy to take the time to really hear what our souls are trying to tell us, or we are too busy listening to our lower-self to hear God. When we do not hear or listen to our soul's needs, we often feel disharmony in our bodies and lives.

When we are actively engaged in our spiritual practices (journaling, meditation, silent prayers, relaxation, contemplation, etc.), we are able to empty ourselves of our concerns and focus on the needs of our souls. In order to better allow the Spirit's white light to surround you and focus your hearing, you may want to light a white candle containing sage oil. This candle will help purify the air. Such moments have often brought insights for me. For example, recently, in November of 2009, I was sitting in silent contemplation, drinking chamomile tea, listening to soothing music and burning a white candle. All at once, a thought came to me to order $300 worth of *Poise for the*

Runway of Your Life. It was noon on a Thursday. I am a massage therapist who never knows how much I will make from one day to the next. By the end of that day, I had made $220. By 11 a.m. the next day, I had earned the rest of the money and was able to purchase the books. I thank God for allowing me the mental capacity, physical health, and strength to work in order to accomplish the task of buying the books.

St. Teresa of Avila

St. Teresa of Avila stated in the 16th Century that our minds are like "an unbroken horse that would go anywhere except where you wanted it to." During meditation, we can retrain our minds to adhere to a deep state of relaxation, which creates an improved mental state. Is your mind an "unbroken horse?"

I have seen on talk shows that researchers have found that when we journal, we improve our immune systems and calm our nervous systems, heartbeat, and respiration. Journaling your thoughts can help relieve stress, which can relax your entire body. As such, if you journal daily, you may gain magical insights into your life.

It is December of 2009 as I write this chapter to you. It is cold and gloomy outside. As it is the end of the year, it is a great time to conduct a life review to see where you have been and where you are traveling on your runway.

A life review occurs when one looks back on his or her life and does an assessment to see what he or she has accomplished. What will you carry into the New Year? It is not necessary to wait until the end of a year to create a life review. You can do one right now! Can you commit to doing a life review for the past year in order to see where you have grown?

It has been said by many masters that it is "about the journey, not the destination." This statement means that what you have learned and incorporated along your runway is more important than reaching the goal at the end. What positive inspiration can you share with others? In my third book, *Poise for the Runway of Your Life*, I explain the process necessary to maintain balance and poise while traveling on your spiritual and personal runway. Your poise is determined by the successes in your life and your ability to recover from a crisis or transition in a positive way.

Meditation

Take a couple of cleansing breaths. Breathe in through your nose and exhale through your mouth. Focus on your breathing. It is a cold day, outside and indoors. Every time you breathe, you see your breath in the air. Your entire body becomes relaxed – your head, face, neck, shoulders, stomach, butt, legs, and feet. Now, sit in a calming posture, smell the essential oils of orange and lemongrass. The orange oil will remove any depression from your mind. The lemongrass will renew your spirit and soul. Look back over the past 12 months. Do not go further back. What do you see? What have you achieved during each month or each quarter? Have you followed your dreams and innermost desires?

Look at each of the activities in your life. Are there some that you would like to re-do or never repeat? If so, let them go. Surrender your life and heart to God. Do not let anyone but God and yourself influence your journey. What do you want to do on your journey? As the snow falls from the sky, see your dreams in the snowflakes. Each dream is falling into your soul, bringing it nourishment and life.

Stop thinking and simply sit calmly. Focus on your breathing and seeing your breath in the air. Know that God is present everywhere and living within your soul. God is approachable and ready to assist you when you need help on your runway. You just need to ask. Be clear about your intentions, needs, and desires. Expect a positive outcome and wait on God's hand. Let go of the decisions about how and when something will happen. Learn to surrender your dreams to God. Just know that "It is done unto you as you believe" (Matthew 9:28, KJV). What do you believe? So be it.

Vibration Cooking

Herbal Tea for Relaxation

<u>Ingredients</u>

7 leaves of lemon balm

1 lemon

1 cup of water for each cup of tea that you wish to brew

Handful of spearmint leaves

2 tablespoons of raw honey

Squeeze one lemon into the water. Bring the water to a boil in a pan. Add the seven lemon balm leaves and a handful of spearmint leaves. Boil for five minutes.

Pour into a cup and enjoy! I often add two tablespoons of raw honey as a sweetener to the tea. I grow my own herbs and use them dried or fresh.

Chapter 12

Measuring Your Success

"All achievements, all earned riches have their beginnings in an idea."

– Jeremy P. Tarcher, The Prosperity Bible (2007)

Good morning, readers. Today is December 16, 2009. It is 8 a.m. and I am writing in hopes that I can help you to develop a clearer understanding of how to measure your personal success. As I try to tune into your vibrations, I have two white frankincense candles burning and soft music playing in the background. I am asking the Spirit for assistance in communicating to you about the secrets of success and what you need to become successful.

We all have our own ideas of what success means. As I write, I am setting my intentions, desires, and expectations for this chapter. It is my deepest hope that this chapter allows you to obtain insights from individuals who have come down the runway before you and to gain a clearer understanding of the secrets of and how to obtain success. What's cooking within your soul? Is success what you want to behold?

Just as you would pull out the necessary utensils and ingredients to make gingersnaps within your kitchen, so must you put together the correct ingredients and utensils to create success within your soul. You must follow clear directions in order for your baked items to come out right. Let your soul be your life's kitchen.

How do you measure success in your life? Can you smell your success? Are you afraid of success? Does it remind you of the gingersnaps baking in your soul? What do you smell as you progress down your runway? So often people measure success by what others deem successful.

Do Not Look outside Yourself for Answers

We often look outside of ourselves for answers in order to reach our inner and ultimate goals. I have done this over and over again. Have you? For instance, I know a man who makes a good living and has many expensive material goods that he prides himself on owning; however, he looks at life as being half empty, never half full. As such, he complains constantly. He has been married for 20 years, has two children, and drinks heavily. Although married, he has three girlfriends spread across the city. He works a 12-hour shift at the railroad every day and receives excellent compensation for his overtime, yet he complains constantly about his work. Every night, he returns home and complains about his co-workers. If success comes to one of his co-workers, he feels the need to one up them in any way possible. In addition, he owns several rental properties. His tenants do not always pay their rent on time, which makes him unhappy, but he fails to do anything about it. Do you think that he is successful in his life? Is he fulfilled? Is he fulfilling his Divine purpose and meaning?

How Important Is Success to You?

Do you measure your success against the success of others or are you satisfied simply by achieving what God wishes you to achieve? What is your Divine purpose? Do you know? Use the space below to express what success means to you and how you measure it. _____

_____
_____
_____
_____
_____
_____
_____
_____
_____
_____
_____
_____
_____

How Do You Start Your Day?

Every morning, when I wake, I repeat an affirmation. My positive affirmations were given to me by God when I moved to Carrollton, GA. The majority of the time that

I lived in Carrollton, I did not know where my next meal or paycheck would come from because I had not yet built my list of clientele and I did not know my Higher Power. Despite this stress, I used that time to deepen my faith and trust in a Higher Power. I used the affirmation below and it got me through. Now, I would like to pass it on to you:

I have prosperity, abundance, success, health, and happiness in my life.

As you say the affirmation, believe in the words and you will draw all of the things that you need to become successful into your soul. You never know when you will encounter a piece of information or a person necessary to fulfill your destiny. Always keep your eyes and ears open for God's power and message.

Maybe You Are Not a Businessperson

Remember that you do not need to be a businessperson to achieve success in your life. As long as you are undertaking your true purpose, you are following the will of the Spirit and you will achieve success.

According to *Webster's New World Dictionary* (1997), *prosperity* is defined as "wealth or an economic well-being" (p. 378). I define prosperity as good fortune. Therefore, when I talk about prosperity, I am referring to being able to receive good fortune in my life, such as wealth, good health, and well-being. John 1:2 of the New Testament states "Beloved, I wish above all things that thou mayest prosper and be in health, even as thy soul prospereth" (KJV). I believe that God wishes us to be prosperous and have good fortune in our lives. One must have a prosperous state of consciousness to draw prosperity to one's life.

The same dictionary defines *abundance* as "more than needed" (p. 3). I define abundance as an overflow from the universe. My definition is why I have included abundance in my affirmation. I feel that every day of my life is a day of thanksgiving. My cup runneth over with the bounty of the universe. I have allowed my heart, soul, and mind to become open to receiving this overflow.

The online *Encarta Dictionary* defines *success* as "an achievement of something planned or attempted; an attainment of fame, wealth, or power; something that turns out as planned or intended; and someone successful, wealthy, famous, or powerful because of a record of achievement." When I think of how I measure success in my life, I know that I must be in a prosperous state of consciousness in order to bring success to my life. Within my soul, I know that everything that I touch will grow, develop, and flourish.

What's Cooking in Your Soul

Journal Your Thoughts about This Chapter _____

_____
_____
_____
_____
_____
_____
_____
_____
_____

When I Wake

When I wake in the morning, I say my personal affirmation and allow a prosperous state of consciousness to overtake me. Then, I know that I will have a successful day. When you believe that you will be successful, your life will become successful. Simply keep your mind in tune to the Creator of all things and you will be able to claim your blessings of success.

How Is Your Health?

Health is a part of the affirmation that I invited you to say. Let's stop to ponder that word: Health. It's been said that health is not a commodity to be bargained for. Instead, it has to be earned. A few years ago, I decided to take personal responsibility for my well-being. At the time, I was trying to re-create myself so that I could model and fulfill my destiny. Many religious teachers and spiritual healers have taught that sickness starts in the mind and works its way into our bodies. Once you declare that you are healthy, your mind tells your body and soul that you are healthy. Can you state that your body does not contain sickness within it?

Whether you are able to state that you are free of sickness or whether you are working toward that goal, you should practice preventative health measures. By coupling these measures with your spiritual practices, you can protect your body and soul from sickness. "Let your food be your medicine and medicine be your food," Hippocrates said. Often the simple act of eating healthy foods can cure your disease or sickness. For example, when I have a runny nose, I add three cloves of garlic and a pinch of fresh ginger to the vegetable juice that I drink daily. This combination stops my nose from running.

In order to be happy, you must rely on your inner self and not outside sources of stimuli. During the past few years, I have experienced much sadness within my life and, eventually, went to a doctor to discover the root of the problem. He stated that my sadness was caused by a hormonal imbalance. Hormonal imbalances cause much suffering for those inflicted. I have suffered from this imbalance since I was 20 years old. Now, I am over 50 and every day is an inner battle. One day, I will be up in spirit, and the next, I will be down. The best way to describe these emotions is that most days feel like nights when all of the lights are turned off within my soul. Some call this the "dark nights of the soul." I believe that my imbalance was created, in part, by my unconscious desire to hold on to old concepts, people, places, and things that I should have let go of. Once I was diagnosed, I took the opportunity to assess my soul in an effort to discover its true needs and what needed to be let go of in order to allow myself to become healthy and move forward.

In order to correct these imbalances, I began taking herbal and vitamin supplements, started receiving massage therapy once a week, continued to exercise, and began eating even healthier. Most importantly, I decided to focus on myself and no one else. Then, I took control of my own happiness and let go of the old aspects of my life that were cluttering my soul. I desired success and sought to achieve it. Determination, joy, and success became my mantra.

Learn to Start Your Day with Positive Affirmations

In order to bring success, health, and balance into your life, you should start your day with a positive affirmation.

Please use the below space to create a positive morning affirmation for yourself:

_____
_____
_____
_____

And so it is….

Say your affirmation once in the morning and see what happens in your day. Journal your feelings below. Next, continue journaling your feelings in a notebook specifically set aside for this purpose. It is my hope that once you begin journaling, you will continue throughout your life.

Day 1

_____
_____
_____

Day 2

_____
_____
_____

Day 3

_____
_____
_____

Day 4

_____

_____

_____

Day 5

_____

_____

_____

Day 6

_____

_____

_____

Day 7

_____

_____

_____

Continue this process for 30 days. It is my belief that if you journal for 30 days, you will be more inclined to continue journaling for the rest of your life.

Education and Success

I recommend that you read *The Prosperity Bible* by Napoleon Hill, et al (2007). This book contains historical accounts of a number of individuals who became successful using the world's greatest secrets to achieving wealth and prosperity. In addition, I would like to suggest that you read *Think and Grow Rich* by Napoleon Hill (1937), as it contains the secrets of how to become successful in your life in spite of your social and economic standing.

In 2008, my church decided to conduct a prosperity class because of the recession. The book that we used was based on *Spiritual Economics* by Eric Butterworth (2001). This book provides valuable information about how to use spiritual principles to increase your finances and teaches that we were born into prosperity through our birthright from God. In light of this, I decided to gain a better understanding of the contents of this book and the recession facing our country. I headed to the public library. The recession has been a curse to some and a gift to others as those of us who wanted to re-create ourselves and our professions were allowed the time necessary to accomplish this task.

I requested *The Prosperity Bible* and *Spiritual Economics* from the library as well as additional information on recessions. Once I began reading *The Prosperity Bible*, I could not put it down. In fact, I renewed the book so many times that I could not renew it again. At that point, I decided to purchase the book for my own personal collection. Now, I have purchased both of the above books for my personal collection.

Discoveries within *The Prosperity Bible*

From *The Prosperity Bible*, I learned that many master teachers and successful people came from poverty situations during financial depressions. They used their humble beginnings as the basis for their hunger for success. This hunger allowed them to become successful and provided them with a desire to share knowledge on how to gain prosperity in the midst of nothing. Each of these individuals became a successful millionaire. The majority of the 500+ individuals within this book were able to create prosperity in spite of a lack of education, family or outside support, and/or little or no money. They were able to succeed because they discovered the secrets of how to become successful and wealthy using the power of their minds. Once they became successful, they became willing to share this knowledge.

Before we move on, I would like to ask how many of you are stuck in place simply because you do not believe that you can become successful. If you answered in the affirmative, then you need to remove "I can't" and "I won't" from your vocabulary. Replace these phrases with "I can" and "I will."

Within this great book are hidden messages describing how to use the secrets in order to gain success. There is a Zen proverb that states, "When the student is ready, the teacher appears." Open your heart and mind in order to reveal the truth of the secrets. Become one of the many men and women who have had their lives changed by this simple truth. The first 185 pages of *The Prosperity Bible* contain information from Napoleon Hill's book *Think and Grow Rich*.

In the preface of *The Prosperity Bible*, Jeremy Tarcher states that

> Riches cannot always be measured in money! Money and material things are essential for freedom of the body and mind, but there are some who will feel the greatest of all riches can be evaluated only in terms of lasting friendships, harmonious family relationships, sympathy and understanding between business associates, and introspective harmony, which brings one peace of mind measurable only in spiritual values. (Hill, et al, 2008, pp. 5-6)

In 2008, shortly after I began studying this book, I was asked to give a presentation to the West Georgia Realtors Group. I chose the topic "Forget the Recession: Create Your Own Destiny" and used some of the stories within *The Prosperity Bible* as examples within my presentation. In the next section, I will share some of these examples with you and how I related the 13 principles to my purpose of reclaiming my childhood dreams to write and model!

The 13 Keys to Success

Each of the men and women used as examples within *The Prosperity Bible* believed in the 13 principles. These principles are important to the secrets of success.

1. **T**houghts are Things

Napoleon Hill affirmed and taught that once our thoughts are combined with a purpose, persistence, and burning desire, they can be converted into money and material goods. For example, I had a thought that I wanted to be a model. I combined this thought with a desire to model. I persisted in this dream and it became a reality.

2. **Desire**

The first step toward riches and success starts with desire. What's cooking within your soul? Do you have a desire for success? Or are doubts, fear, and worry causing your success soufflé to fall flat?

3. **Faith**

You must have faith in your ability to be successful. You must be able to visualize your desires in order to achieve your destiny. Faith is a "state of mind that may be induced by auto-suggestion" (Hill, et al, 2007, p. 38). Once I entered modeling school,

I coupled faith in my success with auto-suggestion and made my childhood dream a reality.

4. **Auto-Suggestion**

   Your personal affirmations are your auto-suggestions. If you fix your thoughts on what you would like to achieve, you will be able to achieve it.

5. **Specialized Knowledge**

   Each person has general and specialized knowledge. It is your specialized knowledge that will help you to succeed. If you lack the specialized knowledge required to allow you to succeed, you should seek out others who have this knowledge in order to help you carry out your "plan to action." The idea that you should use a "Master Mind" group to gather the specialized knowledge required to succeed was developed in the 1800s and has progressed in leaps and bounds since that time, thanks, in part, to the ability of the people within this book to utilize the secrets. Please see number 10 on this list for more information on "Master Mind" groups.

6. **Imagination**

   Albert Einstein was a physicist most famous for his theories of relativity for which he won

What's Cooking in Your Soul

the Nobel Prize. He is also famous for stating that "imagination is far more important than knowledge. For knowledge is limited to all we now know and understand, while imagination embraces the entire world, and all there ever will be to know and understand" (Thinkexist.com). The ability to imagine something must be present before one can create something. Before entering and while in modeling school, I would sit and visualize myself in ads. Now, I am a print model! That is, I do commercials, pictures for newspapers, brochures, and such.

7. Organized Planning

In order to move ahead with your desires, you must have a plan to action. Henry Ford became successful when he developed an organized plan to action for and did not give up on the creation of the V-8 motor.

8. Decision

Many of us fail to become successful because we postpone important decisions or make poor decisions instead of taking the time to examine all of our options. "Procrastination, the opposite of decision, is a common enemy which practically every man must conquer" (Hill, et al, 2007, p. 103). When putting a plan to action into place, you should consider what you want from your plan and then put it into place. Once you make a decision, stick by it, and move forward. Do not let others delay your decision-making process.

An example of a decision that I had to make was whether or not to attend modeling school. I almost did not attend simply because of the monetary cost of the education. I was the breadwinner in my household and did not know how I would find the funds to attend. After searching my heart, I went to the school to find out more about its programs. At that time, I discovered that not only did the school offer student loans, but I also qualified for one! Suddenly, my place in the school was assured, simply because I had made a decision to find out more information about the school and its programs.

9. Persistence

You must be persistent in pursuing your dreams. If you allow setbacks and mistakes to stop you, you will never achieve your goals. Have faith and apply it.

10. Power of the Master Mind

The *Master Mind* is defined as the "coordination of knowledge and effort, in a spirit of harmony, between two or more people, for the attainment of a definite purpose" (Hill, et al, 2007, p. 124). This process requires you to work with others to achieve your dreams. For example, when you read a book, do you realize that the author did not work alone? He most likely relied on others for help in the compilation, editing, and publication of his book. It is my belief that all authors, even bestselling authors, seek assistance from others in order to shed light on how to improve their work. I know that I rely on a host of people to equip me with the knowledge and skills that I do not possess in order to succeed.

11. The Mystery of Sex Transmutation

Do not be afraid of the word transmutation. It simply means a change from one form to another. Hill refers to sexual transmutation as a "switching of the mind from thoughts of physical expression of human desires…to thoughts of some other nature" (Hill, et al, 2007, p. 128). Once a person gets a burning desire within his soul to create his dreams, he will experience the discovery of imagination, courage, willpower, persistence, and creative forces that he never knew existed within his soul.

12. The Subconscious Mind

Your subconscious mind knows your deepest desires and beliefs. When you practice faith and utilize affirmations, your subconscious mind will recognize these positive forces and begin making positive changes within your life.

13. The Brain

Drs. Alexander Graham and Elmer R. Gates observed that every human brain both broadcasts and receives vibrations of thought (Hill, et al, 2007, p. 149). When starting on a new project, I first visualize what I want to create, a process very similar to viewing a painting. Then, I create the project.

"Success comes to those who are success conscious."
– Napoleon Hill

Henry Ford

Henry Ford is credited with producing the V-8 engine. According to history, he saw the need for a new type of engine. After explaining his vision to his engineer, his engineer told him twice that it could not be done. Ford insisted that it could and, six months later, the V-8 engine had been created. His persistence revolutionized the auto industry.

According to *The Prosperity Bible*, many people make the mistake of assuming that because Ford had little "schooling," he was not a man of "education" (Hill, et al, 2007, p. 54). However, this mistake occurs because they do not understand the true meaning of education. Education is derived from the Latin word "educo," which means to draw out and develop from within. According to Ford, a man is educated if he "knows where to get knowledge when he needs it, and how to organize that knowledge into definite plans of action" (Hill, et al, *The Prosperity Bible*, 2007, p. 55).

Ford created a Master Mind group to help him locate the specialized knowledge that he needed to become one of the richest men of his time. This practice has been carried out throughout history. Sometimes such groups are called "brain trusts." They help powerful men and women make decisions.

Ford prided himself on his persistence. Although he started life poor and uneducated, he did not give up on his dreams. Instead, he used the information within his mind to make his dream a reality.

Florence Scovel Shinn

Spiritual teacher and metaphysical writer Florence Scovel Shinn was born in New Jersey in 1871. Before becoming a successful author in her own right, she illustrated children's books. The first book that she authored, *The Game of Life and How to Play It*, was self-published in 1925 because she could not locate an interested publisher. Being self-published during this time in history was highly uncommon and most people would have simply given up on their dream, but since Shinn had the necessary persistence, she was able to succeed in achieving her dream.

She believed that life should be looked at as a game and not a battle. Given the correct understanding of the rules, one could successfully navigate the game. The rules, she believed, were based on the Old and New Testaments of the Bible. One of her favorite quotes was "Whatsoever a man soweth, that shall he also reap" (Galatians 6:7, KVJ). She used her desire to get published and become a successful author.

Tai Chi

To help remove your fears about achieving success, try the centuries-old Chinese martial art, Tai Chi. While its roots can be found in Chinese medicine, the West has adopted it for its healing and relaxation qualities and its ability to strengthen movements. Do you wish that you had more flexibility, muscle strength, and endurance? If so, then this exercise is perfect for you as it improves these three areas. For that reason, it is also recommended for individuals with arthritis. Further, it also helps to calm stress and remove the symptoms of fibromyalgia.

Meditation

Are you afraid of achieving success? Most of us are more afraid of success than failure. Begin today to challenge that fear and welcome acceptance.

Light a white candle in order to invite God into your life. Light a stick of Spiritual Perfume incense in order to enhance your spiritual consciousness and awareness of God. Focus on the light and love of the Spirit. Sit or lie flat on your bed or couch. Relax and let go of your day. Forget everyone and everything. Visualize the light rays from the Spirit as they beam a bright white light. Can you see the light? Be one with that presence. Feel its warmth. How do your soul and spirit feel? Do they feel light, warm, and blissful? Do you feel chill bumps down your arms and spine? God is present everywhere that you are. Know His presence. Accept His presence. There is nothing to be afraid of when in His presence.

Success is your birthright. Each of us has been bestowed with unique gifts. While we have the freedom to choose our career paths, families, and friends, God guides our runways, ensuring that we have opportunities to utilize these gifts. We should not compare our lives to others, only to that which we can achieve. Ask God to help you achieve success based upon the gifts provided to you and the runway that you have chosen. Accept His guidance and you shall be successful! So be it.

Affirm that you and God are one. There is nothing to fear. Success is already yours; claim it. Believe in your success, feel it, and know that successful people are being attracted to you each and every day. Give thanks for the success that you have already achieved in your life. Amen.

Vibration Cooking

Gluten-Free Ginger Snaps

I am allergic to flour that contains gluten. Thankfully, there are many alternatives to such flour, including soy flour, rice flour, tapioca flour, whole wheat flour, unbleached flour and gluten-free white flour, available at most grocery stores. I normally do not use measurements, but for this one I do!

<u>Ingredients</u>

½ cup of blackstrap molasses

2 handfuls of brown sugar

1 handful of soy flour

Pinch of salt

1 handful of rice flour

1 handful of Bob's Red Mill tapioca flour

A pinch of baking soda

A pinch of ginger

A pinch of cinnamon

¾ cup of cooking oil

¾ cup of water

Preheat your oven to 350°. Grease a cookie sheet.

Mix together the cooking oil, molasses, brown sugar, soy flour, and salt. Mix in the rice flour, tapioca flour, water, baking soda, ginger, and cinnamon.

Roll the dough into 1-inch balls. Put the balls about an inch apart on a greased cookie sheet. Flatten each ball with a spatula. Bake the cookies for 12 minutes.

Chapter 13

The Plants Speak: Yes, You Can Pamper Yourself

"And God said, Behold I have given you every herb bearing seed;
which is upon the face of all the earth, and every tree, in which
is the fruit of all tree yielding seed; to you it shall be for meat."

– Genesis 1:29, KJV

As a holistic body worker and lifestyle coach, I see and feel the grief, desires, pain, and joy of my clients. I love my clients! It appears to me that we do not give ourselves permission to nurture, develop, or foster an inner relationship with our spirituality, our God-self. We do not have to be wealthy in order to pamper ourselves.

May I ask you some questions? Do you understand what pampering, serenity, and self mean? I am going to define the words for you as found in *Webster's New World Dictionary* (1971). *Pampering* is defined as "being overindulgent" (p. 339). *Serenity* is defined as "undisturbed or calm" (p. 429), while *self* is defined "as with oneself" (p. 427). Please take a moment to answer the questions below.

1. How do you take away your stress each day?

___
___
___
___
___
___
___
___

What's Cooking in Your Soul

2. Do you ever take time to have a spa moment at home or at a professional establishment?

_____
_____
_____
_____
_____
_____
_____
_____

3. Do you enjoy soaking or relaxing in a warm tub filled with aromas or herbs?

_____
_____
_____
_____
_____
_____
_____
_____

4. Does your spirit need to reconnect with your soul?

Can you afford *not* to pamper yourself?

_____
_____
_____
_____
_____
_____
_____
_____

You are probably wondering what the purpose of a pampering moment is. Well, it helps you to reconnect, balance, and place your spirit back into harmony so that you can face the days ahead. It also reduces your stress level so that you can cope. We must unlock and unblock our spirits and pamper ourselves so that we can give our best to our lives.

Please repeat the following affirmation:

I will learn to pamper myself. I will learn to pamper myself today. I will take the time to pamper and reconnect. I love me. I will become one with myself. I will nurture, protect, and pamper my spirit today! So be it.

What's Cooking in Your Soul

Scientists and researchers have shed light on the benefits of meditation, visualization, and prayer. Meditation allows your spirit to block out distractions and helps to calm the mind. This practice is simple enough to undertake almost anywhere at almost any time of the day. You can meditate while washing dishes or staring out a window. Or you can sit cross-legged on the floor, couch, or chair and think about how to resolve the issues in your life. I meditate by sitting still and thinking about nothing. Then, if a question pops into my mind, I focus on it, allowing my inner voice to answer the question. One of my friends meditates by staring at candlelight. The only condition of meditation is that you must be still and listen to your inner voice. It is also beneficial to use the aromas of sage, lavender, patchouli, rosemary, and sandalwood to help promote a serene, soothing, and energetic meditation.

Let the Plants Speak

The plants listed above want to talk to you. They can be used to renew one's spirituality and inner-self. Let the plants speak:

Sage

All herbs have Latin names. My Latin name, according to *Making Plant Medicine*, is *Salvia officinaltis*, which means "to save" (Cech, Cech, & Gunter, 2000, p. 204).

I was used as a nervous system tonic in medieval times to calm those who were sick. I help people focus inward on their grief, insomnia, and depression. My incense helps purify the air in homes. According to *Dian Dincin Buchman's Herbal Medicine* by Dian Dincin Buchman, placing a pot of my tea in a sickroom will help control germs as well as help deodorize and maintain odors (1996, p. 28). I am often found in gardens and can be used to help with many illnesses and conditions. I can be made into a tea to lift your spirits. If you add a pinch of cloves to the tea, I can help fight your depression.

I am used to cleanse teeth and control bad breath by applying the dried version of myself to your toothbrush. This is one of Carol's favorite methods of cleaning her teeth and mouth!

You can use me in a tea rub or bath to help lower high fevers. I can also be used as a poultice, which is a raw or mashed herb applied directly to the body to heal bruises, loosen congestion, reduce inflammation, or draw pus from putrid sores and toxins from infected areas (Buchman, 1996, p. 301).

Carol often rubs my oil on her clients and burns my scent in a candle.

Lavender

It is my job to bring comfort to those who suffer from one or more of the following conditions: manic depression, exhaustion, and nervousness. My scent helps promote relaxation and balance within one's home or body. Some people use me as a dryer sheet by placing my leaves in their dryer with their wet clothes.

Patchouli

I am often used to provide relief by releasing pent-up emotions, nervousness, and depression by applying my scent to an individual's temples or using my oil as a massage lotion. My scent is intriguing and warm. I am often put directly on the body or in the bathtub during a long soak.

Rosemary

You will never believe all of the good things that I can do to help you get through the day. I am used to stimulate energy, improve memory, and boost confidence, perception, and creativity. If used in a homemade scrub of sea salt, water, body or olive oil, and my scent, I will awaken your senses.

I am also an antiseptic, a headache dispeller, and medicine for your heart! Many people who practice folk medicine believe that I am a cure-all plant.

Not only am I an herbal medicine, but I am also a garden aid. Bugs in the garden fear me, so I am often planted near vegetables.

Sandalwood

If you love to meditate, you will love me. I am often used in Nag Champa incense. I have been used in religious ceremonies for centuries because I help to ground you, while at the same time open you to your higher self. Carol loves to use me as incense when she writes or meditates. You will, too!

Dandelion

Everyone thinks that I am only a troublesome weed in the yard! I have fooled them. I am really a wildflower and a useful plant. Many people eat my bitter leaves in salads during the spring. I am often mixed with other plants to provide relief for muscle pain and backaches. I even have a positive affect upon the female organs. Carol's grandma loves to use me for her family just as Native Americans have done for centuries.

I am both medicinal and cosmetic. In *Dian Dincin Buchman's Herbal Medicine*, Buchman states that the "barefoot doctors" of China use me for healing purposes (1996, p. 30). Sometimes my tops are crushed, simmered, and placed on breast abscesses. I can be used on a long-term basis to strengthen the body after illness as I help build blood and strengthen your liver. I am good to drink with honey or milk. Many people use me as a stimulant for the scalp by adding my oil to their hair products. I am often used in tandem with toothpaste as a breath freshener, with skin products as a tonic, or with teas or salads as an immune system booster (Buchman, 1996, p. 29-30).

After Carol had her fourth child, she developed Hepatitis C, which often causes cirrhosis of the liver or liver cancer. She began drinking carrot juice to aid in healing her liver because it has been shown to strengthen liver cells. Then, she learned that dandelions can be used to stimulate and cleanse a sluggish liver.

Carol's paternal grandmother was a full-blooded Cherokee Indian. Every morning, she would dig up the root of the dandelion, boil it, add honey, and give it to her children to drink. Carol still drinks a dandelion tea twice a day each day every other month.

Aromatherapy

Aromatherapy is the use of essential oils from aromatic plants to help someone become relaxed, balanced, rejuvenated, and restored. This process is also used to enhance the body, mind, and spirit. Hippocrates, the father of medicine, said that the way to health is to have an aromatic bath.

Ancient Egyptians used aromatic oils for their total well-being and closely guarded their secrets as to how to mix their medicines and perfumes. Even Cleopatra relaxed in essential oil and milk baths to keep her skin looking great. Often, when Egyptians were buried, they had perfumes and blended fragrances placed with them in their tombs.

Citrus scents, such as lemon, orange, grapefruit, and tangerine, are often used in diffusers during the morning hours because they help create an uplifting home and joyful workspace.

Essential oils affect the body, mind, and spirit. According to the *Aromatherapy Handbook for Beauty, Hair, and Skin Care*, they stimulate metabolism and transmit neuro-chemical messages to organs, glands, and lymph nodes via an individual's sense of smell (Keller, 1991, p. 19). These oils are antiseptic, fungicidal, bacteriostatic, and antibacterial, which means that they kill germs and prevent the growth of bacteria and viruses.

Meditation

Yes, you can pamper yourself! Give yourself permission. Stop whatever you are doing. Turn off the radio or television. Place your favorite aromatherapy oils on your temples and sit in a posture of gratitude or lie on the bed or floor.

List below what you are grateful for in your life.

_____
_____
_____
_____
_____

What would you like to see change in your life?

_____
_____
_____
_____
_____

I see you walking into a field in the dead of winter. The wind is blowing, pushing you toward the river. You see your parents sitting on the river bank waiting to communicate with you. Be open with them about how they treated you growing up. You tell them your side of the story. They listen and understand what you are trying to tell them. They apologize for mistreating you. You have been released from this negative emotion. You take off your coat and do not feel the cold. You begin to run. You are happy and emotionally free from the damage caused by your childhood. You smell the sage of the field as it helps to release your negative emotions.

Now, the sun is higher in the sky. You spot a deer in the distance. It runs into the woods because it is free. You smile as you look up into the sky and see a flock of birds singing and flying. Your heart becomes warm. The birds bring you a message from God. They tell you to wake up. Love yourself and learn how to pamper your soul so that you can continue your inner healing. You have a lot to give to your family, community, and friends. Write and tell your story, share it at your church, give of your talents, go back to school, help animals and children, live and create your dreams.

Through prayer, forgiveness, self-empowerment, exercise, the creation of a journal, knowledge of the power of herbs, the practice of aromatherapy, participation in massage or bodywork, silence, meditation, church attendance, participation in a good diet, the practice of gratitude, and creative thinking, you can live a God-centered life. Such a life is called a spiritual practice. So be it.

Bonus Recipe

Carol's Creamy Skin Care Cream

1. Get a book on herbs or weeds and their use. Identify the herb *Plantain* in your yard (not the fruit). Most folks think this plant is a weed, but the leaves, roots, and seeds can be used for healing.

   Plantain has big leaves that may be used for healing the outer layer of the skin. I have used this plant on hives, earaches, cuts, beestings, and other problems on the outside of the skin. Don't eat it, though!

2. Take this plant by the handful and place it into a quart-sized mason jar. Top with olive oil. Put the jar with the weed and oil away in a dark place for two months.

3. After two months, purchase beeswax, essential oil of lavender, shea butter, cocoa butter, and small jars from a craft store.

4. Next, use an old saucepan that you don't want to use again. Cut the beeswax with a sharp knife about the length of three fingers together. Put the wax into the saucepan.

5. Strain the oil from the jar and put aside.
6. Once the wax is melted, add the oil, a handful of shea butter, 12 drops of essential oil, and one small stick of cocoa butter. Stir.
7. After 20 minutes, remove the mixture from heat. While still hot or warm, pour the cream into jars. Seal the jars once the cream has cooled.

Vibration Cooking

Rosemary, Sage, and Orange Oil

Ingredients

10 rosemary sprigs

10 -15 sage leaves

2 oranges

Canola or olive oil

Zest the two oranges. Make sure to grate a little as you zest in order to enhance the flavor.

Preheat the oven to 300° and then reduce the temperature to the warming setting.

Place enough oil in the bottom of a two-quart pan to cover it. The amount will be based on how much oil you wish to make. Place all of the ingredients into the pan. Cover the pan with the lid. Place the pan in the oven for two hours on the warming setting.

After two hours, remove the leaves and the seeds from the oranges. Strain the remainder of the oil mixture into clear jars.

After the jars have cooled, place them in the refrigerator.

I use this oil when I am baking lamb chops or roast beef. I even put it on my garden salad and raw and cooked vegetables.

Chapter 14

Are You a Late Bloomer?

"What is a weed? A plant whose virtues have not yet been discovered?"

– *Ralph Waldo Emerson (1803-1882)*

Have you ever heard the phrase "bloom where you are planted?" Start where you are, just like the small mustard seed that is planted yet will yield one of the largest plants in a garden. What's cooking in your soul? Are there gifts, mysteries, careers, and stories that are untold? If only your truthfulness would unfold.

Do you sense that you have been a weed in your own garden that's planted inside your heart, mind, and soul? This is just the time for everything to be stirred and mixed up and unfolded into what you want it to be. It is your season now!

When you read that statement by the religious author Emerson, what comes to your mind? My dears, your virtues have not been discovered or uncovered yet. Do you think your seeds can be planted where you are right now – where you are in your life? Or do you try to dig up the dirt from the past and give it new life? Do you then try to re-plant dead seeds that cannot bloom? The reason why it can't bloom from the past is because the seeds are dead. They can only bloom when they are planted into the now. Your dreams, once activated by intention, desires, and faith, are the same way.

Preparing to Plant Seeds

It's been said, "A farmer is the biggest risk-taker in the job market." They invest time, energy, money, and faith in their craft. Often they only see failure, but they start over, over, and over again to see the plants grow. I love to watch farmers' plants yield to a harvest from the seeds they plant.

Before farmers prepare the ground, they make a plan to action. Mentally, they see what is needed and make a list of what they should buy from a catalog or hardware store. Often this is done by measuring how much ground they have and how many seeds can be planted. This prep time is given careful consideration. A lot of planning time could also be called meditation, contemplation, and visualization. Seeds and fertilizers are ordered or bought for what is needed to support to the soil's chemistry. The equipment to till the land and all that's needed for that is bought. The time is right, it's two months later, and now it's time to go to work and plant the seeds in faith. Do you guess that the farmer would plant seeds with the mental atmospheres of doubt, fear, and worry – like we do so often? And then we can't figure out what happened to our dreams. We wonder, "Why did they die before the launch?"

The ground is prepared and now it's time to plant the seeds. The deeper you plant the seeds, the more the seed will yield. Roots, as you know, grow very deep and that's where all the nutrients are in the soil. Not at the top. When we plant our dreams, we should carry them deep inside our soul to where the root of Spirit can attach to them. When the dreams are left on the surface, the seeds within cannot root and will wash away with the rains. Is this what you want?

Have you observed a farmer or a person who has fruit trees or vines? They are busy giving added vitamins and minerals to support the growth of their plants. After careful observation, they give a large amount of tender loving care daily. Most trees and vines aren't neglected by their owner. If the weather turns to a freeze, they have to cover the trees and vines when in bloom or they will lose the fruits. The trees or vines must be carefully taken care of, especially in their "blooming season." As I am writing this message to you, the Biblical scripture John 1:1-2 (AKJV), rings clearly through my head: "I am the true vine, and my Father is the farmer. Every branch in me that bears not fruit he takes away: every branch that bears fruit he purges it, that it may bring forth more fruit." Let us stop here and ponder that timely scripture from Jesus, our way-shower. Write your thoughts here about the above paragraphs or not: _____

_____
_____
_____
_____
_____
_____

What's Cooking in Your Soul

Our dreams and heart's desires require the same attention and planning that a farmer gives the land when preparing the soil for planting. We, too, must follow certain steps in order to bring to pass our Divine destinies. In John 1:1, we read that "The Father is the farmer." Since that is true, I believe we are just stewards over the land and our inner dreams. Are you a good Shepherd or Steward of the gifts God the Father has placed inside you to blossom and mind? What can you do better in your creation? For me, even though I write New Thought materials about "life lessons learned," I, too, need to better implement my dreams and goals in order to go to the next level of my journey. My plan to action is to use my time more wisely and to put forth an increased effort for marketing myself and books. You can write your plan to action here.

So be it.

I Missed My Season

Are you one of those people who sense they have missed their destiny? It came and left without letting you know? Often we think "our time" was years ago. Another myth we have is that we are too old to create and to reach our destiny. Are you? Then sometimes we don't want to claim what is our mission to do at the present time. We want to look at another's life instead of doing what we know we should do. We spend our creative time trying to fit ourselves into another person's clothes, car, home, job, bank account, title, education, etc. That energy is so wasted and misused that we "mis-create" our lives. Then we can't understand why we are miserable and unhappy. We have been trying to fit into another's life. In this case, we aren't blooming where we are planted. I say again: actually, we are trying to wear another's shoes and they don't fit ours. Whose shoes have you been trying to wear on your Divine Journey? Do they fit? Are they too big or too small? Pull your own shoes out today and try them on and see what happens as you step into your Divine Destiny.

I am reminded when I look in the field of a garden that blooms are a variety of colors. So are we. The blooms are also many sizes from small to large ones. There are short plants and tall ones like the cornstalk. However, the truth is, we are all God's unique creation, loved all the same. We just need to welcome our uniqueness and give ourselves permission to grow, develop, harvest, and yield our destinies, which are many.

Visualizing Your Destiny

If visualizing is an important act for the farmer, how important is it for us? Before anything is created, it must be seen with your mind's eye. With music, most musicians are hearing with their ears first – before the music notes are seen. I see what I want to create before it's done. Then I have to believe what I see, feel it, and know that it will come to pass in due season.

I love color within the walls and atmosphere of my home. My planning time is right now, I am preparing for spring while in the dead of a cold snowy winter blast in Nashville. There is snow and ice on the ground outside. But, my home and heart are warmed with the God of all creation living inside of me!

I am writing to you, my dear, at 1 a.m. It's very, very cold. A painter has been at my home all morning and he's coming back the next day. Two days ago, I decided to get some Hunter Green paint for my foyer. The other side is Yellow. All I could see when entering my front door was the healing, growth expansion, and natural color of Hunter Green. The paint was bought (my action work), then while I was in the check-out line, a painter was behind me. He gave me his card and I shared with him that I was a massage therapist. He said that he had never had a massage. Therefore, we exchanged our services. My foyer is now Hunter Green and he has experienced a relaxing Swedish massage! This is the Law of Attraction and a process called Mental Atmospheres at work again in my life. It works the same in yours! You must see it, feel it, and then believe, apply faith, and wait in trust that all desires will show up. As long as what we desire is in our highest good, it will be given unto us. Our timing is not God's timing. We must practice patience, much like when baking bread from scratch. We must prepare, wait, and let

What's Cooking in Your Soul

it rise and then place it in the oven at the right time to bake. Wait on the Lord, my friend.

What do you want to create? By when? Don't write about how. What plans do you have? Write them here: __

_____
_____
_____
_____
_____
_____
_____
_____
_____
_____
_____

Amen.

Our Season, Our Right Time

In the book of Ecclesiastes 3:1 (KJV), it is written, "To everything there is a season, a time for every purpose under the heaven: A time to be born and a time to die; a time to plant and a time to pluck up what has been planted." There is a time for your dreams to flourish and yield. You have been in preparation. Seeds that you have planted when you were a child are ready to prosper, bloom, or grow. Can you see it, feel it, and know that this is true? The weeds must be plucked out in order for "new growth" to burst through the fertile ground. Out with the old and in with the new. Make room for expansion and increase by "letting go" of anything that no longer serves your life. You can do it. Make room. I have been giving away anything in my home that I haven't worn in two years and anything that is just taking up space. We want to hold on to people, places, experiences, and things that don't serve us any more. Let them float away into a sea of nothingness. Say good-bye and thank you for the "lessons learned." Then change your mindset to create your newness.

Please ponder this statement written by Ernest Holmes, the Founder of Religious Science, A Philosophy, A Faith, A Way of Life, as stated in *The Science of Mind*:

> Each person has a mental atmosphere which is the result of all that he has thought, said and done, and consciously or unconsciously perceived. The mental atmosphere is very real, and is that subtle influence which constitutes the power of personal attraction, for personal attraction has but little to do with looks. It goes much deeper and is almost entirely subjective. This will explain our likes and dislikes for those with whom we come in daily contact. We meet some only to turn away without a word,

while others we are drawn toward, and without any apparent reason. This is the result of their mental atmospheres or thought vibration. No matter what the lips may be saying, the inner thoughts out speak them, and the unspoken word often carries more weight than the spoken. (1988, p. 350)

Holmes did not receive any formal education. After reading his profound insight, I ask you, what have you been thinking about concerning your Divine Mission? What has your mental atmosphere consciously and unconsciously been thinking about what you know it is you're to do in this life? In the book of Ecclesiastes, it is written "To everything there is a season, a time for every purpose under the heaven." You can attract and draw your destiny to you by the power of your inner thoughts and vibration. There is a time and purpose under your heaven just right for you. In my book *In Due Season: Destiny Is Calling Your Soul* (2007), I wrote about me at age 49, consciously awakening to remember my childhood destiny to model and write books. A theme of *In Due Season* was interwoven inside my heart, soul, and mind as I wrote to the readers. Here is an excerpt from the introduction:

Dearest Reader,

While meditating, creating, and writing this book for you, I held you in my heart and mind. *In Due Season: Destiny Is Calling Your Soul* is an account of my personal transformation and purpose on this earth, the title *In Due Season* comes from the Bible, Galatians 6:9 (KJV), *"And let not us grow weary (give up) while doing good, for in (the right) time we shall reap (yield what we have planted), if we do not lose heart (lose faith.)"* (p. xi)

As you read that verse from the Bible, you can clearly see that one should not give up and get tired. There is nothing wrong with resting your soul and body. Do that often. When you are doing for God, others, and yourself, know that you are on the right path. As you do well, it will keep you focused on your goals. Nonetheless, in the right time you will reap the harvest planted so long ago – as long as you don't give into fear, doubt, and worry. They are defined as lower vibrations and they often create a sickness. These vibrations work to kill or abort your dreams; they are a negative vibration. Then you wonder what happened to your dreams? Your mental atmosphere, a higher vibration, kills or robs them. Not someone else – you did it! *You* kill your dream, no one else. *You* are the dream robber. Stop right now and contemplate how many dreams you have killed by your inner thoughts. Stop rehearsing your past. The curtain is drawn and the event and scene are over. No longer blame others and yourself for mishaps and disappointments. It is time for you to take a personal accountability to own what you did, what you thought, and what you didn't do to start to manifest your dreams. Next, see what you can replace and re-create or create. Believe me, it's not too late, and you are not too old to dream your dreams. Plant your seeds of fulfillment in your life, world, and affairs and watch them do well if you nurture your seeds. Look at the example of the farmer's ways when he or she is about to plant their harvest – apply the same principles and wait. Your dreams are not about money, clothing, and material needs. They are about applying your positive thoughts; right action, imagination, desire, faith, patience, and trust in your God and your God-self. Let's you and I together claim and affirm your entitlement to thrive, grow, bloom, and prosper today and every day. That was a mouthful! Take time right now to stop and ponder.

Meditation

From the book *The Language of Letting Go*, by Melody Beatty:

Timing

Wait until the time is right. It is self-defeating to postpone or procrastinate; it is also self-defeating to act too soon, before the time is right.

Sometimes; we panic and take action out of fear. Sometimes, we take untimely action for revenge or because we want to punish someone. We act or speak too soon as a way to control or force someone to action. Sometimes, we take action too soon to relieve feelings of discomfort or anxiety about how a situation will turn out.

An action taken too soon can be as ineffective as one taken too late. It can backfire and cause more problems than it solves. Usually, when we wait until the time is right – sometimes only a matter of minutes or hours – the discomfort dissolves, and we're empowered to accomplish what we need to do.

In recovery, we are learning to be effective.

Our answers will come. Our guidance will come. Pray. Trust. Wait. Let go. We are being led. We are being guided. (1990, p. 328)

Affirmation from the same book:

"Today, I will let go of my need to control by waiting until the time is right. When the time is right, I will take action" (p. 329).

Before I leave you, I want to share some insights written in my book *In Due Season*, on the topic of Season:

- ✦ In season – at the right time or proper time. May I ask if it is your right time to prepare or to commit to your soul's purpose? Have you defined your soul's purpose?

- Out of season – give interest or character to; make fit for use by a period of keeping or treatment. Many times you must wait out of season so to say, while God is allowing your character to build. This will make you fit for your season and grant you knowledge and insight into your missions.
- Seasoning – something that gives a better flavor or character. Have you noticed that smoke meat tastes better than regular meats? The flavor is the result of an aging process. If you have been waiting like me to live your purpose for many years, your flavor is probably more developed in order to give to others and yourself.
- Last season's ticket – a ticket or pass entitling the holder to certain privileges for the season or a period specified. Your sacred source has a pass entitling you to your privileges, to achieve your life's journey. Open your heart to receive the fit of service to mankind. It's your gift from source to have the right to be happy and to have the joy that comes with serving. (Batey, 2007, p. 72)

Vibration Cooking

A Wholesome Snack

Have you ever bought almond butter from the store? Its texture is like peanut butter. You can eat it on celery, whole wheat bread, a bagel, or an apple. When I am eating light, I just eat it on a spoon. Enjoy!

Chapter 15

The Ending of this Book

*"There I say unto you. What things so ever ye desire, when ye pray,
believe that ye receive them, and ye shall have them."*

– Romans 8:26 (KJV)

Are You Ready for a Spiritual and Personal Transformation?

You are wondering what a spiritual and personal transformation is. Then you may ask "does this apply to me?" No matter what our ages are, we all face crossroads while traveling on our runways of life. *Webster's New World Dictionary* (1991) clearly defines *spiritual* as: "of the spirit or soul; of consisting of spirit; refined in thought and feeling" (p. 454).

In the same book: *personal* means "private; individual; of the body or physical appearance; having to do with character" (p. 352). Now we will explore the word *transform*: "to change the form or appearance; to change the condition, character, or function of" (p. 500). It is my deepest hope that you now have a clearer understanding of what is meant by spiritual and personal transformation.

> *"You don't go through a deep personal transformation without some kind of dark night of the soul."*
>
> *– Sam Keen (1931-); Jerry Brown radio interview, KPFA, Berkeley (California), 19 October 1995*

Where Am I Going?

Often when we become of a certain age we look around and say, "Am I missing something?" and/or "Where am I going?" Some experts would like to call this a "midlife" or

What's Cooking in Your Soul

"identity crisis." We then assess where we have been, where we are going, and what the next steps are to continue on our journey. Maybe we have been stay-at-home parents for 18 years, a professional teacher, pastor, or are seasoned in another profession, and know our passions and desires are to paint our dreams on canvas. Or could it be your 25-year marriage ended in divorce or a death? Nonetheless, it is time to understand where you are going next.

This world's economy (recession), that we are so-called facing has taught many "life lessons" for those who are seeking to turn yet another page in their life. For me, I have learned to look inward for strength to create and manifest the desires that I long to create in my life, world, and affairs. A considerable amount of folks who have been tied down to a 9-5 or 12-hour job are not unleashing their inner creativity, learning to take a risk, or to try something different. There are a few folk that are still spinning their wheels to figure out who they are and where they are going in this life. Most people are looking for changes no matter what their ages are. They are searching for answers to "What's next and how do I get there?" The answers are different for each one of us. They ask, should they learn how to fly an airplane at sixty? A grandfather asks, can I find my true love mate again after 20 years of being alone? Spiritual and personal transformation is about going within your soul to find out what truly defines "who you are." Do you really understand "who you are" and "what defines your soul?"

What are the needs of your soul? When you were working those long hours for another person, you were that corporation. When your parents were alive, you were someone's child. Once you got married, you were someone's spouse. Let's take a moment to reflect: remember when you were at home raising your children, your children's needs came first – "you gave to them first" – or when you were in college when your passions were so fresh that you could taste them, and your zealousness pushed you into action and you would not settle for less than your heart's desire. Spiritual and personal transformation will allow you to feel this way again, and have no doubts about your future success! You will gain a newfound freedom that your soul has longed for for many years. Because once you understand who you are in the image and likeness of God the Father, you will have freedom inside your soul.

Welcoming Changes

"To everything there is a season, and a time for every purpose under the sun."

– *Ecclesiastes 3:1 (Ancient Eastern Manuscripts, AME)*

Changes occur constantly: hourly, daily, monthly, and yearly. We can enter in a posture of grace or resistance, you have to choose. As you create a "spiritual practice" and enter a sacred place for refuge, your challenges can be met in grace; resistance will prolong your transformation. I talk and write about a "spiritual practice" often, however, it consists of:

- Daily communion with your Higher Power
- Journaling your thoughts (fears, doubts, happiness, and successes)
- Meditation along with contemplation: being still in silence
- Eating wholesome foods
- Exercising your body and receiving bodywork such as massage, facial, or reflexology
- Attending a center for spiritual worship or connecting with your Higher Power
- Reading edifying books and enjoying edifying conversation
- Listening to uplifting music and watching positive TV shows or movies
- Adding anything that's positive to your life

This action will help unblock, deny, and hinder all emotional, spiritual, mental, and physical patterns that may obstruct your path to your destiny. Then you can put the pieces back together like a puzzle. Next, create your masterpiece called "My Life!"

Right here, stop and write the masterpiece of what you desire in your life:

_____

_____

_____

_____

_____

_____

_____

_____

And so be it!

In Due Season

In the Bible in the book of Galatians 6:9 (AEM), it states: "Let us not be weary in well doing; for in due season we shall reap, if we faint not."

How many of you have been weary in your life, world, and affairs? Do you feel like fainting? You feel like "what's the use?" Your inner self-talk is "I try and I am getting nowhere on my journey. Why is this happening to me? Life is useless." How many of you have even noticed your inner self-talk? As many of you may know, I wanted to model for magazines when I was 12 years old. I also had the ambition to write and be creative in the visual arts. At 14, I started on that path of my destination without any parental support. I entered a contest for a National Model Search and was a finalist! Once I was 18, I went to Fashion school, which was my inner true passion.

What's Cooking in Your Soul

While I was young I wasn't a "good student" academically – my learning style wasn't present. But in fashion school I made As and Bs. I come from a family background of educators. But that route was never for me – my path was so different. I walked to the beat of my own heart even at a young age! Many of my relatives thought I was rebellious. I laugh now; I just knew what I wanted even at an early childhood age! My inner soul wanted to create art, model, and to write books!

Oh well, after many bumps and mishaps on the road of life, finally, I am intentionally focused on my inner dreams. Life to me is not about the destination of a dream, it's all about the "life lessons learned" on the way. You know that many masters have said that "Life is not about the destination, but the journey." After ending my marriage of 21 years and raising six children, I finally stepped into my dreams. Thirty years later I remembered, and woke up to recapture my childhood dreams, which were to model, write, and use my artistic abilities. But you know I had to remake myself over and heal and change my inner self-talk. My children are all grown, I am free of a life-partner and have done my "inner work" to let go of my past and create my future.

Forgiveness was a big part of my inner healing; it works when you apply the principle. Most people are afraid to apply that posture to "practice the gift of forgiveness." They don't want to "let go" because the pain and the past feel comfortable. You must learn to "move on." I live completely in the now, not in the past and not too far into the future! The things of my past help shape my experiences and future.

Is there anyone you need to forgive? You cannot live one foot in the past with your body heading into the future – it just won't work. This was the start of my spiritual and personal transformation for me. You can do this too, it is for you! With faith, trusting in a Higher Power, changing your mindset, setting realistic goals, and stopping focusing on limiting beliefs, you too can reach your ultimate goals in your life.

Start by asking yourself:
- What are the desires of your heart and dreams? Just *what* is cooking in your soul? Is it fear or faith? Is fear or faith boiling within your soul?
- What were your childhood dreams that you sat and daydreamed of day after day?
- How many fears are holding you back from you stepping into your destiny?
- Are you ready to move forward or are you stuck in the past? Maybe you are too far into the future. Can you live in the Now of today this moment?

Let Go and Really Let God

Churches and centers have sung about "letting go," "releasing," and "letting God" for decades. Twelve-step groups and self-help programs have talked about letting go and trusting in a Higher Power and they give positive affirmations for us to use. We have also created our own positive affirmations to help change our consciousness and start us believing our own thoughts. After a few days, however, we are back where we started in doubts, fears, and worries. Why? Stop here and ponder what happens in the patterns of your life that you return to this place of nothing gets done. Be honest with yourself – go within your soul's stirrings to see why you fall back on what you have always relied on.

I would like to challenge you, my dear, to start to figure out what's cooking in your soul? Are there many stories yet untold? Can you begin to step one foot in front of another to create the desires of your heart? What's cooking in your soul? Now's the time to step out and dream. Once you make that first step, you will only see and find that your Higher Power has already gone before you and opened your path. Your job is to say "Yes" and move into a position of active faith along with confidence and assurance! You can really let go and let God show you the way.

May I advise that you be "poised for the runway of your life!" So be it!

Affirmation

I will this day let go and let God direct and guide my footsteps. I know what's cooking in my soul and will walk boldly into my destiny!

Meditation

As I place my feet on the ground I know that it is Holy Ground. I close my eyes and go to the center core of my being. I take deep cleansing breaths there into my abdominals, up and out through my lungs and throat and out from my mouth. I am relaxed and poised.

I see my God-given destiny, and it's calling my soul. Every day I hear it clearer and see it more clearly. There are footprints in front of my foot that have gone before me. They are big and deep into the earth. I calmly follow the footprints of the Spirit. I say, "YES!"

The way becomes clearer each step I take in faith, trust, confidence, and assurance. I am not alone; the Spirit guides me and I follow. I say thank you God the father and mother. Amen.

Vibration Cooking

Mango, Lemon, Lemon Balm, and Mint Herb Ice

Ingredients

1 handful of raw sugar

Water to fill a two-quart saucepan

4 lemons, squeezed with peels grated

1 dash of lemon flavoring

2 mashed or blended mangos, mixed with lemon balm and mint leaves

Mix raw sugar into the pan of water; bring to a boil over high heat and leave uncovered. Stir often. Take off the stove and stir in the rest of the mixture. Put the ingredients into ice trays or a pan or bowl and cover. Place in freezer and freeze for at least one hour.

I serve this in a bowl or, if I use ice trays, I put it into a glass and pour other drinks on top of it. Serve with a fresh mint or lemon balm. Enjoy!

Dear Reader,

Monday, March 22, 2010

By now you are aware that our time is up. We've now made it into the season of spring in Nashville, Tennessee! What's cooking within your soul? Can you stir and mix up your soul's passions? It's time now to start the process.

It's my fondest hope that "as you believe" in your dreams, they are coming to pass. See them, feel them, and know that everything happens in your mind first.

I have included the song *If You Believe* here to offer you a feeling of hope. Read the words and apply them to your life.

In appreciation,

Author and Lifestyle Coach, Carol S. Batey

If You Believe – Terri Brinegar

I'd given up hope, thought I'd blown my chance for happiness
And I forgot what really mattered in myself
Between a rock and a hard place,
That's where I was

But something inside said don't stop trying, give it time
Where there's a will there's a way, trust in what's inside
And suddenly my heart knew

Just what to do

Now I'm taking time alone
To finally take back who I am
A little voice inside me says:
"Whatever you can dream, you'll be it,
"If you believe."

Starting to live my life with feeling from my heart
Starting to have a little faith in myself to reach for the stars
I know I'm gonna make it
I know what to do

Repeat chorus

Terri Brinegar
(615) 975-5008
info@jukejoint.com
http://www.jukejoint.com/tbones/lyrics.htm

Bibliography

Batey, C. (1996). *Parents are Lifesavers.* Thousand Oaks, CA: Corwin Press.

Batey, C. (2007). *In Due Season: Destiny's Calling Your Soul.* Bloomington, IN: AuthorHouse.

Batey, C. (2009). *Poise for the Runway of Your Life.* Bloomington, IN: AuthorHouse.

Beatty, M. (1990). *The Language of Letting Go.* Center City, MN: Hazelden Foundation.

Browne, S. (2004). *Sylvia Browne's Lessons for Life.* Carlsbad, CA: Hay House.

Butterworth, E. (2001). *Spiritual Economics.* Unity Village, MO: Unity Books.

Buchman, D. D. (1996). *Dian Dincin Buchman's Herbal Medicine.* New York: Wings Books.

Cech, R, Cech, S, & Gunter, A. (2000). *Making Plant Medicine.* Williams, OR: Horizon Herbs LLC.

Encarta Online Dictionary. (2009). Microsoft.

Frank, L. (1998). *Random House Webster's Quotationary.* New York: Random House.

Forward, S, & Torres, J. (1986). *Men Who Hate Women and the Women Who Love Them.* New York: Bantam Books.

Guralnik, D. B. (1970). *Webster's New World Dictionary* (2nd ed.). Cleveland, OH: World Publishing Company.

Guralnik, D. B. (1971). *Webster's New World Dictionary* (2nd ed.). Cleveland, OH: World Publishing Company.

Neufeldt, V. (1991). *Webster's New World Dictionary* (3rd ed.). New York: Simon and Schuster.

Neufeldt, V. (1997). *Webster's New World Dictionary* (3rd ed.). New York: Simon and Schuster.

Holy Bible King James Version. (1976). Nashville: Thomas Nelson.

Holy Bible New King James Version. (1979). Nashville: Thomas Nelson.

Hill, N. (2003). *Think and Grow Rich*. New York: Jeremy P. Tarcher/Penguin.

Hill, N., et al. (2008). *The Prosperity Bible*. New York: Jeremy P. Tarcher/Penguin.

Holliwell, R. (1964). *Working with the Law*. NP: Fashion Press.

Holmes, E. (2007). *The Science of Mind Textbook*. NP: BN Publishing.

Holmes, E. (1991). *The Ernest Holmes New Thought Dictionary*. Camarillo, CA: DeVorss & Company.

Holmes, E. (1998). *The Science of Mind*. New York: Jeremy P. Tarcher/Penguin.

Ingham, E.D. (1984). *Stories the Feet Can Tell thru Reflexology*. St. Petersburg, FL: Ingham Publishing, Inc.

Jordan, E.B. (2006). *The Laws of Thinking*. Manchester, CT: Foghorn Publishers.

Keller, E. (1991). *Aromatherapy Handbook for Beauty, Hair, and Skin Care*. Rochester, VT: Healing Arts Press.

Morehead, A. & L. (1956). *New American Webster Handy College Dictionary*. New York: New American Library.

Trine, R. (1897). *In Tune with the Infinite*. New York: T. Y. Crowell & Company.

Walsh, N. D. (1996). *Conversations with God*. 1996. New York: G.P. Putnam's Sons.

The World Book Complete Word Power Library. (1984). Chicago: World Book Encyclopedia.

Photograph by Gene Smith

About the Author

Carol S. Batey, author of *Parents Are Lifesavers* (Corwin Press 1996), *In Due Season: Destiny's Calling Your Soul* (AuthorHouse 2007), and *Poise for the Runway of Your Life* (AuthorHouse 2009), is committed to spreading information about how one can improve and renew the purpose of one's soul by providing coaching workshops and speaking at seminars for anyone who wants to step into their destiny.

Carol has worked as a Parent Involvement Consultant for the Metropolitan Nashville (Tennessee) Public Schools and received national recognition from educators for her work on parent involvement. During the 1992 school year, she was nominated for the J.C. Penny Golden Rule Award, an award given to individuals who have performed outstanding service to the local community, and the school won $1000.

Born and raised in Nashville, Tennessee, Spiritual Lifestyle Coach Carol Batey is the mother of six adult children, and the author of numerous magazine and newspaper articles. Carol was educated in the Nashville Public Schools system, and has obtained multiple Associate Degrees in business from various schools in Nashville.

Carol, at 51, is a Lifestyle Model for Elite Models in Atlanta and a talent of Sharon Smith Talent. She teaches and has worked in the performing arts on assignments. Her "Your Destiny Awaits You" workshops are very popular, and attendants leave with knowledge, motivation, and instruction and a sense of self-empowerment.

She welcomes your e-mails or personal calls, for speaking, coaching, retreats, or workshops for your organization or yourself. Contact Carol via carol37076@aol.com; (615)-485-4548; or her website: www.artlifestylecoach.com. Carol would like to know how this book impacts your life, world, and affairs.

Be not afraid of life.
Believe that life is worth living,
And your belief will help create the fact.
 – Williams James Namasté